Yarns from My Shepherd
Stories to inspire Christians
and of life on The Good Shepherd Farm

by
Michelle Dumoulin

Dedication

To Granny, who taught me to sew, knit and crochet and helped me to become a Proverbs 31 woman who looks for wool and flax and works with my hands in delight.

To my children, grandchildren, family, friends and readers - that you may know Him more intimately.

And especially to my husband Gary, who encouraged me to write.

To God be the glory.

Table of Contents

Preface

Have you ever heard God's voice? I have. It happened in December 1993.

I awoke one morning and started my prayers when I heard the Lord speak to me. "Write". Uncertain, I asked "What ???" Then, His voice thundered. It was so powerful, it was a command! The next time, He bellowed. *"W R I T E !"*

Obediently, I leapt out of bed. "OK Lord". Like many of you I had a morning routine, but not that morning. When I jumped out of bed, I immediately grabbed paper and a pencil and began to write.

The final product was a short story interspersed with poems. It was extremely deep and very personal. I don't even want to read it now as it pertains to a very different time of my life. But, I wonder, what was its purpose? Why did God want me to write that story, and for whom?

I remember sharing it with very few people. One was a man from church who came to my house with his wife to help me understand the Bible. He later told me that my story, tucked away in a Bible he carried in a backpack, was stolen from him. Over the years, I've wondered if God really commanded me to write that story for a thief?

As I prepare to write this book, I am reminded of His thunderous voice once again. But, must I revisit the memories? I don't want to, but I have to. So with trepidation, I respond.

"OK Lord."

Introduction

Writing a knitting book was my husband's idea, but writing this book was mine.

In regard to knitting, I would not consider myself a "master" knitter, but I often receive compliments on my knitting, especially my fair isle knitted items. In this book I will describe the steps of making yarn as well as my fair isle knitting method. I want to share with you my experience and method of creating hand knitted items from fiber animals raised on our Good Shepherd Farm. To begin with, my husband, Gary and I raised sheep and angora rabbits. I card, spin and dye the animal fibers into yarn and then design and knit garments. But creating hand spun knitted items is what I do for pleasure and not my only passion.

Through short stories, I am going to tell you some amazing ways that God has encouraged me throughout my life. As you will see, I am blessed, because my faith and belief in God is established because He chose to prove Himself to me. These stories are very personal and most have never been shared with anyone before, but I am drawn to tell them now. I plan to insert them, not in a chronological order, but rather through some common core or point of view to the fiber process. It is my hope that they are a testimony to the truth and greatness of our God and a source of inspiration to you.

Some of these stories occurred twenty to thirty years ago and I am telling them from my memory. They have not been embellished; they are true. Unfortunately, these are only some of the personal encounters I've had with God. I wish I had kept a journal, but then there would be too many stories to tell!

In the preface, I told you that God once spoke to me and to pique your interest, I will tell you that He spoke to me again. It is my prayer, that as you read this book, you too will be blessed.

Chapter 1

Learning from Granny

It seems totally appropriate to start the first chapter of this book telling you about my grandmother. After all, she put the first set of knitting needles in my hands. But, as you will see, she taught me so much more.

Everyone called her Granny, and although she was constantly surrounded by grandchildren, in my mind, I spent the most time with her. Granny lived directly across the street from my elementary school, and I will never forget climbing those stairs with my brothers and sisters for lunch. Not only did she make the best tuna fish sandwiches in the world but the smell of her baking was a welcoming aroma. On our lunch table she set out our sandwich, a piece of fruit and a glass of milk. If we ate it all we could have a cookie or a delicious frosted cinnamon roll. We always ate it all.

In addition to my lunch time visits I spent many evenings there too. As we sat side by side in her dining room where I was taught most of my lessons, there was often a feeling of loneliness in the room. I knew why. The day my grandmother gave birth to her ninth child, her husband died. She raised her six sons and three daughters the best way she knew how, by putting her trust in God. I vividly remember the photographs, lined up in a row on a side table, of her sons dressed in their military uniforms.

Whenever I felt the heaviness in the room was too great to bear, I asked her to tell me their names again. She pointed to each photo and reminded me. Then, she went to her bedroom and returned with the Bible she kept on her bedside table. I sat there quietly listening to her pray for them and then, once her burden was lifted, we returned to our lessons.

For my first lesson, she taught me to cut bulky wool yarn into small pieces and knot them over a coat hanger to make dusters. Once she taught me to crochet, we also covered them with stitches so garments could be hung without creasing. She taught me to embroider and do needlepoint, but the majority of my lessons with Granny were sewing lessons. She taught me how pins needed to placed properly when laying a pattern to cloth. Before I was allowed to cut the fabric, she inspected every pin placement. By the time I attended junior high school, I made most of my own clothes. Over the years, into my early married life, I made many bridesmaid, prom and wedding gowns for others. I was so skilled with the needle that my hand stitches were nearly invisible. If lace or beads were added to a garment, you would never see the thread that held them in place.

In addition to being a meticulous teacher, Granny was frugal, and I learned to be frugal too. While mom and Auntie Carrie sat in her kitchen eating hot cross buns and drinking tea, I was assigned to the other room to wrap the leftover pieces of yarn into balls or cut scraps of cloth into acceptable shapes for future use. Granny used those tiny pieces of yarn to make the centers of crochet Granny Square afghans and I still have one that I treasure because it was made by her. One Christmas I had very little

2

money for presents for my own children, so I pieced scraps from clothing they had outgrown together with other fabric and made them each a new bed quilt. They loved those quilts so much and would carry them from their bedrooms to the living room to use while watching television.

I remember that I did not like being corrected by Granny, but over the years I have learned that what I considered the most difficult lessons are still valuable to me today.   I understand that scissors are damaged when you try to cut through a pin and scraps of yarn and cloth should not be discarded. I now understand why she was particularly cautious as she taught me to make my first velvet and satin dress. The material was extremely expensive and one mistake could render the fabric useless. A single drop of water on either of those fabrics will leave a permanent scar. And, because of her training, I do not consider a project completed until all of my "housekeeping" is done and every thread or piece of yarn is properly secured and then trimmed.

Granny tried to teach me to knit, but I complained. I complained that she wanted me to wrap the yarn around my neck because I didn't like the warmth or feel of it. Nor did I want to make a hole in my blouse to hang a pin on the shoulder area to run the yarn through. None of that made any sense to me at the time, but I now know what she was doing. She was trying to teach me to knit in the Portuguese style method. Fortunately for me, she didn't give up. Instead, she took me to the City Mission, now known as a community center. There I was taught by a stranger to knit using the English style method. In this method, yarn is wrapped around the needle using the right hand. Recently, I taught myself to also knit using the Continental method, where yarn is wrapped using my left hand. Unfortunately, I regret, that I don't know how to knit using the Portuguese method. In hindsight, I think that Granny felt inferior with her knitting abilities and that her method was strange. But in fact, her style of knitting is still being learned by knitters today and is considered an excellent method for speed while reducing pain in the wrists and hands.

I wish I could go back and repeat my lessons with Granny, because I now know the value of those lessons. I wish she could taste my flaky pie crust or grape jelly, and hope she would be proud of me. I wish that when I became an adult I had asked her more questions and listened more often. I wish I could thank her and love her all over again because now I realize how much she taught me and how much she loved me. But we all know that we can't go back in time, but what we can do is pay it forward.

About ten years ago I was teaching in a local high school and I used that job as an opportunity to be an example of Granny to my students. Although most of the other teachers used their free periods to correct papers or plan lessons, I recognized that time with the students was valuable, so my classroom preparations were done at home in the evenings. Students came to my room to learn knitting, crochet or just to talk, feel safe or seek guidance. On the last day of school, I was surprised and honored to receive a crocheted afghan from one of those students. She had worked on it diligently every night, and by the expression on her face, I know she poured her love and gratitude into each stitch.

4

Recently I devoted a great deal of time to knitting gifts for my nieces and future daughter in laws. More importantly though, while knitting each item, I prayed my heart out for each recipient and at night I also shed tears as I prayed for them to be blessed. When my gifts were finally presented at our annual Women of Faith Conference weekend, I included a scripture verse to summarize my prayers for them and guide them in the future. God has heard my prayers, and one of them is now seeking God first and attending church regularly.

So I hope you have come to learn the many ways in which Granny influenced my life. Although she taught me to sew, crochet or knit for pleasure, more importantly, she taught me to pray without ceasing.

Proverbs 22:6 Train up a child in the way he should go,
Even when he is old he will not depart from it.

My Granny

Chapter 2

Did I Say That?

When Granny got older and became more frail she lived with my parents. One day, when I telephoned my mother, she told me that Granny wanted to leave. I rushed to speak with her to try to convince her otherwise.

I remember sitting across from her and listening to her tell me why she could not live there any longer. She was very sad, but could no longer tolerate my father's constant hurtful remarks. I knew first hand the difficult battle Granny was facing. Many times my father had said things to me that had made me cry. But, at the end of our discussion, I left her room defeated, because she was adamant of her decision. She came down the stairs a few minutes later and I was standing alone. As she slowly walked past me, I said to her, "You know Granny, its real easy to be a Christian when you live in a closet."

She stopped, looked at me and nodded, but I was totally confused. I knew those words had never been processed through my brain. Rather, they had come directly out of my mouth. I stood there in unbelief and asked myself, "Wow, did I just say that to her?"

Fortunately, later that day, I learned that Granny decided to stay, but it wasn't until a few weeks later that I understood where those words had come from. While I was sitting in church listening to a sermon, the pastor said that although he prepares his sermon in advance, he is often surprised by the words that come out of his mouth. Many times, when he preaches, he is shocked by what he says and asks himself, "Did I just say that?" He explained to us that, in fact, it is not his own words, but it is the Holy Spirit speaking through him. And I knew then that the Holy Spirit had spoken through me.

Every now and then I think of that message of the closet, especially when I know I am going to encounter someone whose personality is a challenge to me. In today's society we are constantly told that we should tolerate others who are different or have different beliefs than our own. But being a Christian outside of the closet tells me that I must do much more than tolerate them, I must love them. With my own strength I cannot do that, but with Christ I can!

After going through a horrific life lesson, my response and approach to others is slower, and I am more patient and kind than in the past. A few years ago, I had to interact with someone on a routine basis who frequently made remarks that I found offensive. Every time I entered that building for our meeting, I asked God to help me love her. He did, and others noticed too! God used that struggle to demonstrate a Christlike response. As a result, others who witnessed my response improved their relationship with her as well.

The Holy Spirit also helps me to listen to others more deeply and be compassionate. Many years ago, I attended a church that offered a course on listening and I think it was the most valuable course I ever took in my life.

In the course, I learned that people use key words when speaking that best describes what type of learner they are and how they communicate with others. People who use the word "feel" learn best by physically interacting with the subject matter. If you hear someone say, "I see what you're saying"; they are visual learners and learn best if you draw them a picture. Others use the term, "I hear you". They can easily learn by reading and focus on listening carefully to words being spoken.

During my brief teaching span I incorporated all of these methods into my lessons to cover the various types of learners. And, in an office where I previously worked, this course was helpful as well. At times, an employee unknowingly irritated her coworkers because she repeated what she was being told, as if she was mocking. I explained to them that she was a "hearer" and was only able to grasp an understanding of what was said by repeating it. My explanation helped to heal those relationships.

Most importantly though, I've learned that words speak what the heart feels. While listening carefully in a casual conversation, I sometimes hear the other person make a comment that instantly tugs at my heart. It may be a harsh or negative remark which they quickly try to contradict or ignore and just continue speaking. But, if I gently pursue it, I often find there is a deeply rooted hurt which is being expressed through those words. My compassion can help heal those wounds.

God has also challenged me to forgive people who have hurt me, some terribly. Although I preferred to avoid them and live in my closet, God repeatedly brought them back into my life because He wanted to ensure my forgiveness was complete.

Of all the many things Granny taught me, I can say with certainty the most important lesson is this, "the real challenge in life is being a Christian outside of the closet."

Matthew 12: 34 For the mouth speaks
out of that
which fills the heart.

Chapter 3

How I Became A Yarn Snob

A few years ago, I finally understood why my mother was closest to my sister Becky when we were growing up. They both loved to shop. Although Mom would always ask me to join them on the shopping trips, I refused, because I hated shopping. Unless, of course, it was to shop for cloth or yarn!

My absolute favorite outing was to go to either Thomas' Fabric Store or Maria's Store on Rivet Street with Granny and Mom. We stood in front of the yarn selections and I nearly drooled over all the choices. Yarn was always chosen first by weight, then by color. Yarn weights, or thicknesses, range from lace weight to super bulky and it is extremely important to select the yarn that will yield the correct number of stitches per inch that you are trying to achieve in your project. Granny was always right by my side helping me to make the correct purchase and Mom always helped me choose the prettiest colors.

The only yarn type we ever purchased was acrylic, which is a synthetic fiber. It works well for garments that will be washed frequently, such as afghans, and acrylic yarn comes in a large variety of colors. The sport weight yarn is soft and works well for baby items. But, it is a cheap yarn, and eventually, I had a strong desire for a better quality.

About 15 years ago I was crocheting an afghan for my son. I had purchased some green and maroon acrylic yarn and worked ornate stitches into the design. Although the afghan was coming out beautifully, I mentioned to my husband that I was disappointed. The yarn was so cheap. As I was crocheting, I could actually hear a squeaking noise and it just felt like plastic.

My husband asked me why I wasn't making the afghan out of wool. I responded that, first of all, wool is costly and I would need a lot of yarn for an afghan of this size. Secondly, I told him that wool requires special washing instructions and wasn't suitable for an afghan which would be used daily or washed frequently. Rather, wool is best suited for specialty items such as sweaters, hats or mittens that can be hand washed. To my surprise, Gary said that I could afford wool, if we raised our own sheep. Soon after, my future was changed and we started our Good Shepherd Farm.

I rarely use acrylic yarn now, and if I do, it is of a better quality than in my younger days. Most often, I hand spin my own yarn or purchase higher quality yarns when I can get them at a reasonable price. My hand spun yarn is made from either wool shorn from my own sheep or wool purchased at fiber events.

Depending on the project, I may add angora, mohair or cashmere to the wool. The angora fibers came from shearing my German Giant angora rabbits. These added fibers make the yarn extremely soft and luscious.

When my twin grandsons were born, I knit them sweaters from 100% angora yarn that I spun and then dyed a beautiful powder blue. I added small white rabbit shaped buttons down the

12

front to compliment the sweaters perfectly. The hospital nurses said that I won the prize for the most beautiful baby sweaters they had ever seen. They are heirloom pieces and my daughter in law treasures them.

I love color too, and dye most of my fiber. Sometimes I spin fiber that I have dyed. Other times, I dye it after it has been made into yarn, depending on the final result I am trying to achieve. There are many different dyes and methods of dyeing. While I prefer to use natural dyes, such as Kool-aid, food coloring, plants or teas, sometimes, I need to use chemical dyes to get the exact color I need. I have special dye pots and utensils that are used only for dyeing and not in food preparation.

To add pizazz to the yarn, a metallic thread called angelique fibers can be spun with the fiber. This adds sparkle to the yarn. Beads knitted into a garment add a nice touch too. When planning my final product, I take into consideration many factors, including fiber content, color and added texture.

Wool from different sheep vary in quality as well. There are a number of breeds of sheep bred for their fiber quality, while others are bred for meat purposes. Many other animals provide fiber for yarn as well, including alpaca and llama.

So I guess I'm just not ashamed to say that I am now a yarn snob because I create specialty yarn for most of my knitting projects. I enjoy spinning fibers to produce yarn which is really soft and now, knitting is extremely enjoyable.

Proverbs 31:13 She looks for wool and flax
and works with her hands in delight.

A Knitted Shawl from Hand-spun, dyed, Corriedale Fiber

worn as a shawl

worn as a scarf

"My Love Flows"
Original Knitting Pattern by
Michelle Dumoulin

This scarf was designed to offer a beginner in knitting an opportunity to create a luxury garment piece. After knitting it myself, I believe even an advanced knitter will love the results.

After searching through hundreds of stitch formations in my knitting encyclopedia for an attractive design formed by using only a knit stitch, I fell in love with the "Garter Drop Stitch". Also, an important feature in this scarf is the "Double Garter Stitch Selvage Edge". It ensures the scarf lays flat and doesn't roll into a tube shape.

If you know how to cast stitches onto a needle and knit, then simply follow these instructions to complete the design. The detailed instructions are listed to specifically assist the novice, but can be ignored if you find them unnecessary.

Some of you may have purchased my knitting kit for this design, but if you are buying the yarn separately, use fingering weight yarn to achieve the proper fabric drape.

The Knitting Kit includes:
- 3.5 oz, 262 yards, 80% Acrylic 20% Alpaca Yarn
- Hand Made Goodshepfarm Knitting Needles Size 10.5
- "My Love Flows" original knitting pattern

1. Cast on 30 stitches LOOSELY.

2. The selvage edge: The <u>first</u> 2 stitches and the <u>last</u> 2 stitches of **EVERY** row are **ALWAYS** the same to create a beautiful flat garment edge.
    - The <u>first</u> 2 stitches...
        1. Slip the first stitch through the back loop, (see photo A)
        2. Then, knit the next stitch normally
    - The <u>last</u> 2 stitches of every row should be knit normally

Photo A
Slip the first stitch, through the back loop, off the left needle and onto the right needle.

16

3. Now let's add the drop stitch pattern:

- Rows 1 - 4:
    - First 2 selvage edge stitches, (slip one through back loop, knit one)
    - then knit 26 stitches,
    - then knit the last 2 selvage edge stitches normally.
    To simplify, Slip the first stitch, and knit the rest!
    (30 stitches on the needle count)

- Row 5:
    - First 2 selvage edge stitches, (slip one through back loop, knit one)
    - then knit wrapping the yarn twice around the needle (see photo B),
    - then knit the last 2 selvage edge stitches normally.
    (56 stitches on the needle count)

Photo B
Wrap the yarn one extra time around the needle.

Make the knit stitch using the second wrap.

- Row 6:
  - First 2 selvage edge stitches, (slip one through back loop, knit one)
  - then knit 26 stitches, letting the extra loop drop (see photo C),
  - then knit the last 2 selvage edge stitches normally.

    To simplify, Slip the first stitch, and knit the rest!

    (dropping the extra loop formed on previous row)

    (30 stitches on the needle count)

Photo C
Knit the first loop, then
drop the second (extra) loop.

4. Repeat this 6 row pattern as many times as possible, but remember to leave a few yards of yarn at the end for the bind-off. I was able to repeat the pattern 48 times. Your tension may vary a little from mine and our number of repeats may differ, but it doesn't matter.

5. Bind-off using the following method to ensure the cast-off edge is not puckered.
   - Insert needle in front to pick up 2 stitches (see photo D)
   - Wrap the yarn around the needle clockwise and knit the two together loosely
   - Return that stitch to the left needle and repeat until only one stitch remains.

– Slip the tail through the final stitch and tighten the loop.

Photo D
Insert the right needle in front,
then wrap the working yarn **clockwise**,
(knitting the two stitches together)

6. Housekeeping:
Weave in the tails. Hand wash the garment in warm soapy water, with little to no agitation, using a little dishwashing liquid or shampoo. Rinse carefully; do not allow the garment to hang wet, but rather, squeeze the scarf with your hands to remove the water. Then, lay the scarf onto an old towel, and fold the towel loosely. Drop the towel to the floor and step on it to remove the excess water. Lay the scarf on a flat surface to dry.

"My Love Flows"

Jeremiah 31:3
*"I have loved you
with an everlasting love"*

19

Chapter 4

Heaven's Sound

Hearing the sound of heaven is more magical than any yarn I could ever create or even imagine. How would I know? Because I've heard it.

I was a single parent for many years, and like Granny, I could never have done it without the Lord. If there is one thing I know my children remember about growing up, it is seeing me in prayer. My alarm clock was set for at least an hour before I needed to wake them up in the morning so I could roll out of bed and drop to my knees. Also, I spent time in prayer before I crawled into bed at night. I can't remember a time when I was closer to God, as He heard my prayers of adoration, confession, thanksgiving and petitions.

A few years ago I had a strong desire to re-establish that quality prayer time. But, now I am married to Gary, who is a truck driver. His sleep is critical for his own safety and others on the road. Setting an alarm clock to wake up before him would disrupt his sleep and is not an option for me. So I simply prayed about it and made my request known to God.

Miraculously, the Lord heard my prayer and every morning He automatically woke me up at 4:30 a.m. Upon waking, I looked at the clock and smiled and thanked Him. Then, when I took my first breath, the Holy Spirit would fill me, and I proceeded to commune with God.

This routine became a pattern and continued for about a month. I hadn't given it any thought on the day I travelled out of state to visit my mom. As I laid down to sleep in my bed there, I was exhausted from traveling as usual and fell asleep quickly. When I opened my eyes again, I stared at the clock on the bedside table. It read 4:30.

I smiled and immediately thanked Him for waking me up at that time and I acknowledged that He was a God of the universe and not limited to anything about me or my location. Then, I rolled onto my back, took my first breath, closed my eyes, and began to pray.

Immediately, I was filled with the Holy Spirit more than ever before and in just a moment I believe I was taken to a heavenly realm. All I could see was light, but it was not blinding as it is when staring directly at the sun. Rather, it was a comfortable soft glow that filled my vision. But, I wasn't focused on what I could see. Rather I was completely engulfed and overcome by what I heard.

I knew immediately the words I heard were adoration and praise, but they weren't in any human language. They were long and formed by combining many beautiful syllables together and seemed to go on forever. There were other sounds too that were like music, but not created by any instrument I had ever heard before. The words and sounds were amazing and I was overwhelmed by their magical beauty.

It was such a blessing to stay in that realm for what seemed like just a few minutes, but then the lights and sounds

21

suddenly disappeared. I could now see the walls and ceiling of my bedroom clearly. I wanted to return and immediately tried to remember and repeat the words I had just heard, but it wasn't possible. No sound will ever compare to the praise of heavenly angels.

I continued to lie there for a while just basking in the memory. Then I surrendered to the fact that I no longer felt like I needed to pray. After all, God had just given me the most amazing gift. He knew when I took my first breath upon awakening that I wanted to be in His presence. So He took me high up into the heavens, to a place of amazing worship.

A few years have passed since this happened and I never experienced it again. I understand and accept that it was a precious gift and not a casual occurrence to be repeated.

While some people joke about what they want in heaven, I don't even think about chocolate, colorful yarn or anything else for that matter. I just want to dwell there and worship Him forever, surrounded by those beautiful sounds.

Psalm 57: 11 Be exalted above the heavens, O God;
Let Your glory be above all the earth.

Chapter 5

The Annual Spin-Ins

The weekend after Gary made the comment about raising our own sheep, we were driving through a nearby town and saw a sign at the elementary school that read, "Annual Spin-In". We decided to stop in, and, as we entered the gym, I was excited to see approximately one hundred women with spinning wheels filling the gymnasium floor. There were vendors surrounding the perimeter of the room selling fiber or yarn and we were surrounded by color!

As we strolled around the room, the first thing we noticed was the variety of spinning wheels. Some of the wheels had beautiful wooden spokes while others were a circular solid piece of wood. A few women had hand painted their wheels with bright flowers or pretty colorful designs. We also noticed that some wheels had two foot pedals, while others had only one. All the women had removed their shoes and were treadeling their machines in their stocking feet. One woman was even using an electric spinning wheel.

There was a lot of chaos, talking and laughter and we could see the women were really enjoying themselves. One woman called them all to order and announced that the sock parade would immediately begin. Suddenly, all the women quickly jumped to their feet and formed a line. As we stood on the sidelines, we watched with enjoyment, as they weaved through all the spinning wheels which filled the center of the room, marching in a parade in their stocking feet. All the socks were hand knit from brightly colored yarn they had spun and some were very clever and funny. Everyone was laughing!

When their parade ended they settled back into their seats. We were able to speak with some of them who were friendly and informative. Gary asked them about the different types of spinning wheels and someone told him there was a used Ashford spinning wheel for sale near the stage which would be perfect for a beginner. My wonderful husband purchased that wheel for me along with some fiber. Then, another woman was particularly helpful in demonstrating the spinning technique.

As much as I tried to mimic what they were doing, I was spinning rope! My husband is very smart and actually caught on a whole lot quicker than I did, so he offered me advice. Fortunately for me, a few days later, I went to a home where spinners were gathering and was mentored through the spinning process.

I've been attending the annual spin-in for over 10 years now and each year I try to learn something new. I've learned a lot about dyeing fiber, different plying methods and intarsia knitting from a master knitter. In anticipation of the annual event, I try to save some money in advance so that I can treat myself to something special. Every year, there are different items for sale. Once, I purchased some pretty hand made beaded knitting stitch markers. Another year, I bought an excellent book about dyeing fiber. Most years, I am in search of fiber.

As I mentioned earlier, the fiber from different sheep breeds vary in quality. During the earlier years of attending the spin-in, I was merely attracted to fiber that was fairly inexpensive but dyed bright or pretty colors. As the years progressed, sometimes I went there with a mission in mind.

A few years ago, I was hunting for fiber from a Lincoln sheep. A friend of mine had owned Lincolns and always produced yarn high in luster and shine. I wanted to try spinning some myself and asked all the vendors around the room if they had any Lincoln fiber. Sure enough, a woman had some that wasn't on her display table, but she had brought it with her and just threw it in a box in the corner. I bought quite a bit of fiber for $20 and was really pleased with the spinning result.

Over the years, I've been able to find all types of fiber including Merino, Rambouillet or Corriedale. Last year, I bought Finn which was surprisingly extremely soft.

My husband has been able to attend a few of the annual events if he is not working. I think he enjoys seeing some of the friends I have made over the years. Since we only live about ten minutes away, sometimes, he would just stop in later in the day. One year he really surprised us all with a treat. He had stayed at home and made some malasadas, which is the Portuguese version of fried dough. My friends were overjoyed when he joined my group with a brown bag full of warm fried dough covered in sugar. What a treat and what a thoughtful husband too!

I am fortunate the spin-in is held locally. Some people travel far, from all ends of the State, to attend. I look forward to seeing the familiar faces of friends I've made over the years, but only have the chance to see annually. I get to see a friend who I taught to spin. She raises milk goats and her neighbor has an alpaca farm. Apparently they barter, and every year she proudly wears a new sweater that she knit with her hand spun alpaca yarn. Another friend raises angora rabbits and taught me how to spin angora fiber. A few times, I have met her at local fairs doing demonstrations on spinning angora fiber or holding discussions on the care and maintenance of her angora rabbits.

I've had the privilege of both teaching and learning and look forward to many more years of attending this event.

Since that first year, I purchased another spinning wheel, a Louet brand, which is a workhorse of a machine. But, of course, my favorite spinning wheel, and the one I use most often, is my Ashford.

Song of Solomon 2:16 "My beloved is mine, and I am his."

My Ashford Spinning Wheel

Just for fun I recently painted my Louet Spinning Wheel !

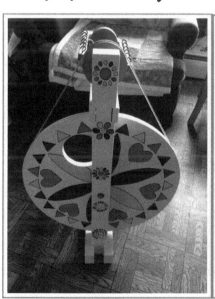

Chapter 6

Dancing In Our Tithes

Throughout my lifetime I've had an opportunity to attend or visit a variety of churches. I was raised and baptized in a Catholic church, but every summer I attended vacation bible school at Granny's church, the Church of Christ. Eventually, I attended the church on a regular basis and was actually baptized there as an adult.

Once, during my school age years, I visited a Jewish synagogue located in my hometown. It was quite a unique experience for me. What I remember most about the Jewish worship ceremony is the singing. While it was all sung in a language I did not understand, I remember that it was beautiful and powerfully worshipful.

I've visited many other churches as well, including Methodist, Presbyterian, Baptist, Nazarene and Pentecostal. What I've learned over the years is that churches themselves were simply buildings where people gathered for worship. Although there is some division, based on religious beliefs, thankfully, the one common thread is Jesus Christ.

One of the churches that I attended was extremely unusual in the format of the service; it was an African Pentecostal Church. Everyone came on Sunday dressed in long white gowns and removed their shoes upon entering the building. Men and women were seated on separate sides of the sanctuary throughout the entire service. The singing was extremely loud and joyful, but the most boisterous part of the ceremony was the presentation of their monetary gifts.

Previously, I told you about the sock parade at the annual spin in, where the women marched gaily through the room, making a presentation of their colorful socks. Similarly, in this church, their was gaiety and joy as each member literally sang and danced down the center aisle, and then offered their monetary tithes.

I've never seen such a beautiful sacrifice of offerings as in this tiny room. It reminded me of King David, who was leaping and dancing before the Lord as the ark of the covenant was brought to Jerusalem! It also reminds me of a song based on Psalm 100 which I can't help but joyfully sing!

> I will enter His gates with thanksgiving in my heart,
> I will enter His courts with praise!
> I will say this is the day that the Lord has made.
> I will rejoice for He has made me glad.
> He has made me glad, He has made me glad,
> I will rejoice for He has made me glad!

2 Corinthians 9:7 God loves a cheerful giver.

Chapter 7

Raising Sheep

Once I learned how to spin fiber, my husband and I continued our discussion about raising our own sheep. Since there are many different breeds, it was important to choose one that would provide the type of wool fiber I desired, as well as select a breed which would survive in the climate where we live. We made a trip to a local book store and purchased a book that described all the different sheep breeds. Eventually, we determined that Romney sheep would be our best choice.

That summer, a coworker took me to her friend who raised Romneys, and there I purchased two females, who I quickly named Molly and Hannah. Soon though, I learned that they actually weren't the best choice, because they came to us with burrs in their fleece, and were very untame. We had never had burrs on our property, but just like dandelions, it doesn't take long for those seeds to spread. Every now and then I still find a burr bush growing which needs to be destroyed.

Shortly after buying our first two sheep, my husband and I went together to visit a farmer from a nearby town who was selling an entire flock of Romneys. The flock consisted of four beautiful females with gorgeous clean fiber, along with a little sister, who happened to be a dwarf. Although that little one would never supply an abundance of wool, I just couldn't leave her behind.

They all stole my heart at first sight and I was so happy when Gary agreed we could buy them all. This time, I took my time and got to know them better before giving them names.

One of them had such gorgeous fiber with long curly bangs that hung down onto her forehead. I named her Corrie because she reminded me of a Corriedale sheep breed with those long curly locks. She was such a sweet girl, who always loved to be petted, and was always my favorite. As it turns out though, the most beautiful fiber came from Greedy, who was named because she always pushed her way through the others to get to the food. It was always easy to spot Greedy out in the field, due to her size from eating so much. But, I think the cutest name of them all was Bonita, which means "pretty" in Portuguese, for my adorable, little dwarf.

As summer progressed, we decided to purchase a ram so the ewes could get bred in the Fall. I'll never forget bringing him home in the back of the pickup truck. By comparison to the girls, he seemed much larger and appeared to fill the entire truck bed! Very quickly I learned that a ram is not an animal to ignore. When the females all came into their heat he was very protective of them. A few times he had me scared out of my wits and I was afraid he was going to charge at me!

The first year of raising farm animals was a huge learning experience for me. Within a year of our marriage, we had moved up to Maine and purchased a 200 year old farm house with 80 acres of land. I had always been a city girl while my husband had been a farmer and everything about farming was new and exciting to me.

31

Although the 30 acre field on our property supplied the hay we needed for the animals, it was a lot of work. First, Gary cut the hay with our farm tractor and mower. Once the hay had dried a bit, he drove the tractor around the field, making continuous windrows with the hay rake. Finally, when the hay was completely dry, it was exciting to see all the bales of hay plop onto the field out of the back of the baler. But then it's really manual labor time, as each bale of hay is lifted onto the truck and then stacked in the barn. In the heat of July, I learned very quickly that hay sticks to hot, sweating bodies, and a good night's sleep is the reward of a hard day of labor.

Cutting the hay was an important annual event, but installing and maintaining the fencing of our four pastures was a lot of work too. Initially, we built what we called a "secure" pasture, which allowed the sheep to exit the barn and roam outdoors freely. The fence was connected to the outer walls of the barn and made of 5 foot high metal fencing and cedar posts. In this pasture, we were certain they were safe from predatory animals such as the numerous coyote that visit our woods frequently. Additionally, we built 3 huge grazing pastures. They were made with electric fencing wire and each pasture was used on a rotating basis. The electric wire and gates limited their access to the allotted pasture and allowed time for the grass to grow in the other restricted areas.

For most of the year, the daily chores were not very difficult and something I could handle on my own. In the early evening, while the sheep were grazing, I cleaned the barn floor and spread some lime and fresh shavings. As I recall, a clean barn is my favorite smell of farming life! Since they were grazing in the pasture, they needed very little hay, but were fed grain in both the morning and evening. Ensuring the sheep had plenty of water to drink was easy during the summer because we connected a hose to fill their water barrel. But, caring for the animals during the winter months was a different story. Gary carried a week's supply of hay bales and stacked them neatly in the barn holding area and we constantly took turns carrying water buckets from the house to fill their trough and kept their water from freezing. The barn floor was allowed to build up a winter pack of hay, which kept the barn warm during the bitter cold winter months.

In the Spring, as soon as they were allowed to pasture, the flock needed some extra attention before the easy summer months began. The lambs born during winter had their tails docked. The ewes and ram were given their annual worming tablets and hooves were inspected and trimmed. But the biggest job for my husband was the shearing.

It was certainly a back breaking job for Gary to wrestle each of them onto their bottoms and remove their winter coats, but I was so grateful as each fleece was stored away and I anticipated spinning the fiber. I had a back breaking job of my own too. Cleaning the barn floor of the winter pack, which by this time, was nearly a foot high, was a physical workout. I was so proud and happy when the floor was once again cleaned. But I think the most exciting time on the farm for both of us was lambing season.

As the summer came to an end, and the weather started to cool down, the girls were usually bred by the ram in October. Since the gestation period for sheep is five months, lambing started in mid February and ended in early March and we waited with anticipation for all the lambs to be born. It was exciting to finally learn whether they were having single or twin births and if the lambs were ewe or ram lambs. Most of the lambs had white fleece, but a few were born jet black. As the black sheep aged, the outer layer of their wool coats faded to a dark brown due to the effect of sunlight.

While some of the sheep were good mothers, unfortunately, others rejected their babies at birth. When the lambs were born, Gary or I would dry them up with old rags and watch to make sure they sucked from their mother. It was extremely important for them to drink the colostrum the mother provided during the first few feedings. We had a few bad ewes that pushed their lambs away when they tried to nurse, and that's when we made the decision the lamb would need to be bottle fed. A powder milk replacer was mixed with water and then warmed and fed to the bottle baby lambs four times per day. Fortunately, I only worked five minutes from home and able to do the lunch time bottle feedings.

Lambing also came with other trials as well. Sadly, we lost our little Bonita, who had accidentally been bred. She was paralyzed when she gave birth to a very large lamb, who also died at birth.

During our first few years of lambing, the winter months had record breaking frigid cold temperatures. I remember once coming home to find Gary with a lamb on his chest, wrapped tightly in his arms as he desperately tried to warm up a frozen lamb. After hours of effort, he successfully kept it alive, but the

34

most memorable of all the lambs was my first bottle baby, who I named Jeannette.

She was my very first black ewe lamb and she was so cute. I favored her so much that I named her after my sister in law, Jeanne, my very best friend. Jeannette was born on a frigid Sunday morning and was rejected by her mother. When Gary brought her into the kitchen, he taught me how to bottle feed lambs for the very first time. We set up the extra large dog crate in the mud room for her, but soon both Gary and Jeannette thought that solution was inadequate and he just let her walk around the house at will. Being a mother of three sons, I told Gary that was not going to work and did the only thing I knew how to do. I went to the local grocery store and purchased infant diapers.

At that time, we had a very gentle yellow lab named Stetson and he became her surrogate mom. Every evening, we all gathered in the parlor, and as the fireplace blazed, Stetson laid in front of it, with Jeannette cuddled up to him fast asleep. In the corner of our bedroom, there is a little alcove where he slept on his dog bed, but he didn't sleep alone.

As we climbed the stairs each night, Jeannette came too, and laid there throughout the night, cuddling with him. Overall, I think our diapered lamb lived in our home for nearly a month, until at last we decided it was time she learned that she was a sheep and not a dog. She lived out in the barn with the rest of the flock from that time on, but always knew my voice.

In fact, they all knew my voice. Just as the sun started to set each night, I would cry out to the flock grazing in the pasture, "Caday, ca-day, ca-day!" and they immediately returned to me, waiting in the barn of our Good Shepherd Farm, for food and safety.

John 10:27 My sheep hear My voice,
and I know them,
and they follow Me;
and I give eternal life to them,
and they will never perish;
and no one will snatch them out of My hand.

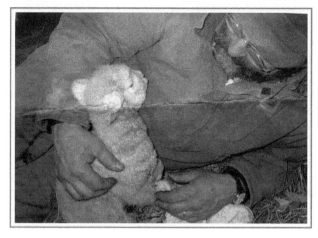

An old photograph of my husband, Gary tending to a newborn lamb

Jeannette, in her diaper, with Stetson !

Some of the flock heading out to pasture

Chapter 8

There Are Many Rooms

There are moments in our life that we will vividly remember forever.

I will never forget when my husband told me that Jeanne died. The details of where we were and how he told me don't really matter much to this story. But, just to tell you how much I loved her, I screamed, from the depth of my soul, I screamed.

And I fought with him too. How dare he say the one person, other than my children, who I loved most in my life was dead? After all, we had only been married a few years, but Jeanne was my very best friend my entire life. Some of you who have lost a loved one may understand, but those of you who have lost someone they really loved will understand even more. But, we also know, that life moves on.

So days, and weeks, and then months passed. And there was only one thing I asked her every day, "Jeanne, why aren't you coming to me?" Let me try to explain.

Soon after my father died, I could smell his after-shave lotion so strongly that I danced with him around the living room, as if I was in his arms. Years prior to that, I had an extremely memorable dream about my grandmother going to heaven shortly after she had passed away. Given those two experiences, I desperately wanted some connection with Jeanne too, and then it finally happened, nearly two years later.

In a dream, my brother Don and I stood in a narrow, rectangular shaped, room. Jeanne was not only my best friend, but also my brother's wife, so it was fitting for him to be standing there with me. At the far end of the room, I saw a doorway, but could not see into the other room, because of the blinding, brilliant light that was radiating from that passageway.

We were standing there for only a moment, when suddenly Jeanne walked through that light and approached us. She was wearing a plain, white short-sleeved jersey, white shorts and sneakers, typical of any other day. We stood there motionless, smiling at each other for a very long time, and basked in the most intense love and joy radiating between us.

Finally, I broke the silence, and asked her heartbreakingly, "What took you so long?"

"I had things I needed to take care of," she said. And, although I didn't understand what she was referring to, I accepted her answer, certain she would have come to me sooner if it had been possible. Then I asked her just one more question, "What's it like?"

Staring intently at me, she said the one and only thing she knew I would comprehend, "There are many rooms."

The next moment, she turned around and departed, walking back into the radiant light, and was out of sight. Once she left, I awoke from the dream and knew with absolute certainty that Jeanne is in Heaven.

There is a scripture verse in the fourteenth chapter of the book of John where Jesus said, "Do not let your hearts be troubled. You believe in God; believe also in me. My Father's house has many rooms; if that were not so, would I have told you that I am going there to prepare a place for you? And if I go and prepare a place for you, I will come back and take you to be with me that you also may be where I am."

Although I've read through the Bible numerous times during my lifetime, that verse was not on my mind that night. I believe the purpose of the dream was for her to use it to give me a message. She didn't specifically answer my question as to what Heaven was like, but told me what was most important.

I am comforted because not only do I know where she is, but she proved to me that Heaven exists! Just like scripture says, she is in our Father's house which has many rooms. And, for those of us who believe in Jesus, He's prepared a place for us too.

There are rooms there for you and me.

2 Corinthians 5:1 For we know that
if the earthly tent we live in is destroyed,
we have a building from God,
an eternal house in heaven,
not built by human hands.

Jeanne talking to Jeannette

Chapter 9

Raw Fleece

Although I found pleasure in interacting with the sheep and caring for them, the main purpose of raising the flock was for their wool. Therefore, keeping their fleece as clean as possible was our goal, and believe it or not, docking their tails really helped to achieve that objective.

For many years, Gary and I attended nearly all of the county fairs across the state. It took a bit of constraint to keep me from heading directly to the barns to visit with the farm animals. We were always repulsed to see some of the sheep on display that did not have their tails docked. Consistently, those sheep had a huge mass of disgusting dung stuck under their tails. On the contrary, sheep with their tails docked never had that problem, and neither did our flock. A few pebbles or small tags were acceptable, but nothing more.

During the first year of attending the fairs, Gary always made it a point to talk with the sheep shearers. He not only discussed the different methods of removing the fleece, but got opinions on various brands of electric sheep shears. Although they are similar to shears at the barber shop, they are much larger in size and heavier too.

In preparation of shearing, we laid tarps down on the floor of our designated shearing area. Of course, we had oil handy to keep the blades sharpened, and a bottle of iodine was nearby, which would be used to stop any bleeding if there were accidental cuts. We kept a full bucket of water close by which would be used to remove the lanolin that frequently clogged the shear's blades. Lanolin is a grease which builds up on wool-bearing sheep and has waterproofing properties. It helps to shed water from their coats and protect their wool and skin from the climate. Lanolin is also used in human skin care products. Sometimes, I enjoyed spinning raw wool fiber because my hands got really soft from the natural lanolin treatment.

I tried using the shears a few times, however, I was apprehensive that I was not holding them at the correct angle to their body. I was petrified that I would pull their skin and cut them. Thankfully, Gary did the job, and eventually, he was able to remove the fleece like an expert. Spinners prefer a fleece which is sheared in one pass, removing long strands of fiber at once. Second cuts, or shorter strands, do not spin well, and sometimes add undesirable nubs to the final spun yarn. Once the best fleece was removed, I would immediately store it in a grain bag for future processing. Then, any second passes from a final trimming were discarded in the trash along with any dung tags that had been originally removed and separated.

I was always eager to start processing Greedy's fiber because she had such long strands of wool which were loaded with crimp. Perhaps one of the easiest ways for me to describe crimp is to think about beautiful wavy hair. Fiber with a fine crimp has many bends or waves, and usually spins into a fine yarn.

Wool strands with less crimp will generally produce a coarser yarn.

To start the process, the fleece was skirted over a thick gauge wire which is attached to some 2 x 4 wood in a rectangular shape about 2 feet by 5 feet in dimension. I looked over the entire fleece and removed any excess hay seeds or burrs and then separated it by quality. The best quality of wool was shorn from the sheep's back, while the neck and belly were dirtier from touching the ground or eating. Any short cuts were removed at this time as well.

After the wool was skirted, I filled a large plastic tub with water from the outdoor faucet. Here, the wool was washed numerous times to remove excessive lanolin and dirt. For the final wash, I added shampoo to the water, and then rinsed it thoroughly clean of any suds. The wool was then placed back onto the skirting table to dry. A slow gentle breeze would really expedite the drying time. Once the wool was completely dry, the fiber was stowed away into clean bags and brought into the house. The skirting table and wash buckets were put away for future use.

Once the shearing was complete, we were well into Springtime and the heat of summer was fast approaching. The view of the pasture changed dramatically because the ewes no longer had their long wool coats and their lambs followed them closely. Just like joy coming in the morning, I loved to watch the gamboling lambs hopping all around their brand new playground, and I was happy.

Isaiah 1:16 Wash and make yourselves clean.
1:18 "Though your sins are like scarlet, they shall be as white as snow;
though they are red as crimson, they shall be like wool."

SKIRTING THE FLEECE

WASHING THE FLEECE

DRYING THE FLEECE

Chapter 10

It's About Grace

Once the sheep were shorn, I couldn't easily identify them as they were grazing out in the pasture. We purposely left curly dreadlocks hanging from Corrie's forehead so I could recognize my favorite. Even Greedy didn't look much larger than the rest of the flock without her massive wool coat.

During the first few days, as they roamed the pasture feeding on the new Spring grass, I always felt embarrassed for them. After all, it was us, their shepherds, who had forcefully removed their fleece and displayed them to the world naked. They couldn't care less and didn't even know they were bare.

But seeing the sheep naked in the pasture always reminded me of when I first became a Christian. As I knelt on the floor next to my bed, tears fell from my eyes onto the open pages of my Bible and my confessions kept uncovering all of my sin and shame. Although I have had that same Bible for many years, I still find the pages which were affected by those water marks. While on my knees, I asked Jesus to forgive me for all of the sins I had ever committed and I was regretful for the many bad or selfish things I had ever done. I kept reading and repeating the words of Psalm 25, asking Him to forgive me for the sins of my youth, and kept uncovering the layers that hid my shameful self.

I am so grateful He did forgive me that day and has not exposed me to the world like my sheep. Rather, the Bible says that He covered me, like flowers of the field, in clothing that is more splendorous than any adornment King Solomon could ever wear.

In addition to praying for forgiveness, I asked God to have mercy on me. I continued to study the Bible and learned that when my sins were forgiven He said they are no longer visible to Him, but rather, they are as far as the East is from the West. In other words, He completely removed my sins from His sight. Then, He granted me mercy and did not punish me for my actions. Once and for all, I was a new creation, born again and my slate board of sin was erased and washed clean. The Good Shepherd, Jesus, had laid down His life for me on the cross and paid the punishment for my sins so that I would not perish.

I am constantly amazed that His love did not stop at forgiveness and mercy and I believe that's why the famous song is entitled, "Amazing Grace". In my heart, I felt like I deserved condemnation, but instead, He gave me a gift called grace. Grace is the blessing of eternal salvation and because of this gift He promised me that I will be received into Heaven, spotless and blameless! How can any gift ever compare to His gift of Amazing Grace? This gift has been on my mind almost daily since I first received it nearly thirty years ago.

Fortunately, about twenty years ago was no exception. I had been carrying some pain and sadness because of hurtful things done to me by a friend. Most often, we avoided each other, but one day found ourselves alone together in the corner of a room at a gathering. She stared at me with repentance in her eyes and said, "You know, it's all about forgiveness." I knew she was sorry for the things she had done and was asking for my forgiveness. I looked directly into her eyes and smiled as I replied, "No, my friend, it's about grace. Grace is so much more. It is forgiveness, with love."

She bowed her head and shoulders with relief, and then nodded to me, knowing that at last we were reconciled. Two weeks later, she died unexpectedly.

Whenever I think of her, I no longer recall her hurtful actions, rather, "It's about grace," echoes in my heart and mind.

Luke 7:47 For this reason I say to you,
her sins, which are many,
have been forgiven, for she loved much;
but he who is forgiven little, loves little.

Chapter 11

Carding The Fiber

My thoughts about the wool that is stored away fill me with anticipation and I am excited to finally have plans for its' use. But, there are still steps in the process that must be completed before I can knit. The wool must be carded to prepare it for spinning. Carding is the process of combing all the fibers in the same direction. During this process, any residual pieces of hay debris are also eliminated as the fibers are pulled through carding combs.

When I first started spinning my own fiber, I used hand carders. They are two individual rectangular wooden paddles that are covered with a cloth made of metal pins. I placed a few locks of the fleece on the left hand carder, and then combed it numerous times with the carder in my right hand by pulling the cards against each other in the opposite direction. Once the fibers were all aligned, I removed the fiber from the pins by holding both carders in the same direction, and slowly combing the fiber off the left carder from the top down, forming a very small rolag. This hand carding process worked fine for my very first project, but eventually my wrists became very sore because I was working them too hard trying to get a large volume processed.

Before long, I did some research about purchasing a drum carder and finally found one available on-line from New York at a reasonable price. My drum carder has two metal pin rollers and a crank handle and it is attached to a heavy table with a screw clamp. This drum carder now processes a larger volume of fiber and is much quicker to use. There are more expensive carders available, which run by electricity, but I could not substantiate the cost of purchasing that type of machine.

On my drum carder, I also blend fibers. Sometimes, I process a few strands of wool, and then I add angora, cashmere, or alpaca fibers directly onto the drum over the wool, and once cranked, they are all blended together beautifully. I love spinning blended fibers because the result is a very soft yarn.

I also blend fibers by color. Sometimes I dye wool in different batches of color before carding. Then, I run one color of fiber through the carder and follow it with a different one. This process makes an exciting wool to spin.

When there is a good amount of carded fiber on the drum, I remove it from the drum with a tool that is similar to a long screwdriver. There is an indentation in the drum for this tool to fit into a slot which lies underneath the wool. I place the tool under the wool and lift it off the drum, then slowly rotate the drum to release the wool from the drum as it is turning. Once the wool is removed from the carder, it is called a batt, which is long and flat with all the fibers generally running in the same direction.

The fiber can also be removed from the drum carder through the hole in a diz. A diz is a tool, similar to a washer, with a center hole. The size of the hole will regulate the amount of fiber formed into long continues strands of fibers.

Since I never know exactly how much yardage the fiber will produce until it is spun, I don't card all the wool needed for the project at once. I card some fiber, spin what I have carded, then card some more as needed. After all the fiber is carded and spun for my project, I clean the drum with a tool that is called a picker. It is similar to a hand carder, but it much smaller. By combing the drum, I remove all the fibers so it is clean and ready for its' next use.

I am so grateful for my drum carder, as I no longer toil to prepare the fiber, but rather enjoy the carding process.

Proverbs 10:22 The blessing of the Lord brings wealth,
without painful toil for it.

Hand Carders

Drum Carder

Batts removed from drum carder

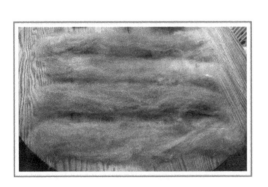

Removing fiber from drum carder through a diz

Dizzed fiber

Chapter 12

All Prayed Out

The wool is carded and all the strands of fiber now lie in an orderly fashion. Unlike the organized fibers of the carded wool, sometimes the trials of life can send my heart and mind into disarray. A heartbreak or problem may temporarily steer me off course from my path, but I've learned over the years to trust Him in every storm.

I've had so many trials in my life and think that is why James 1:2 is my favorite verse in the Bible.

"Consider is all joy, my brethren
when you encounter various trials,
knowing that the testing of your faith produces endurance.
And let endurance have its perfect result,
so that you may be perfect and complete,
lacking in nothing."

Most often, as I go through a trial, my faith is strong, and I trust that God will get me through it. I also know the purpose of trials is to test my faith and see my response to the struggle. I remember some trials that were extremely challenging, but with faith I was able to laugh with joy at the devil when he struck. I told Satan he would be destroyed because my God is greater and always victorious in battle. Unfortunately though, there were times when I tried to fight in battle with my own strength, and I confess, those battles were always lost.

I don't know if you know the story of Job who encountered continuous trials. One day, his enemies killed his servants and stole his oxen and donkeys. Then, fire burned all his sheep and raiding parties took all of his camels. As if that wasn't enough, a mighty wind swept through the house in which all of his sons and daughters were feasting. The house collapsed and all of his children died. While Job maintained his integrity through these adversities, the devil struck him with painful sores from the soles of his feet to the crown of his head. Through all of this, Job was humble and never cursed God about his misfortune. In the end, the Lord restored his fortunes and gave him twice as much as he had before. The latter part of his life was more blessed than prior to his trials.

So there is a summary of Job's ordeals, one significant trial after another. Although I never had the exact same suffering as Job, I've had the experience of facing one problem after another. Fortunately, I've had the same result as Job as well. After passing through storms, I am always blessed, either with an increase in my faith or with a physical blessing.

Approximately five years ago, a nightmarish series of events affected my family and the best way for me to describe it is to compare it to an automobile accident I was involved in years ago. In the middle of winter, I was driving home from visiting my mom with my son seated in the passenger seat of the car. We were already four hours into the drive, just a half hour remained for us to reach home, when I crossed over a bridge. To avoid the cars that were about to enter the highway from the oncoming ramp, I moved to the passing lane and increased my speed. I was now traveling somewhere between 70 and 75 miles per hour, when a tire blew out and the steering wheel began shaking uncontrollably. Using all my strength, I could not control the car, and needed to reduce my speed; so I applied the brakes. At that moment, I lost total control, and at a high rate of speed, the vehicle swerved and crashed into the guardrail on the right side of the highway.

The car still didn't stop. Instead, it spun around, crossed the lanes again, and now facing towards the oncoming traffic, we struck the opposite rail. I remember that specific part of the accident vividly because as the car was spinning out of control I screamed, "GGGOOODDD !"

My vehicle hit the two foot snowbank that covered the second guardrail, flipped on its' side, and rolled over and over and over again. As the car was flipping, my son and I crouched deep down onto our seat to avoid being crushed by the roof. It finally rested on its' tires in the valley of the highway median. I'm sure you can understand that I will never in my life forget his response as I cried out his name, and he replied "I'm OK mom." At last, I was flooded with relief, and my world was right again.

The entire car accident only lasted a few minutes but the nightmare that affected my family was like that collision course by impacting us with trial after trial for years. One day, without warning, our world spun out of our control and we continually crashed into one obstacle after another. When it first began, I screamed, "GOD, Help Us!" With every breath, of every minute, of every day, for years, I begged God to answer my prayers.

At some point, I became exhausted from pleading with God to answer my prayers with solutions which I thought were best. My petitions became nagging and repetitious, as I continually asked please God this, or please God that, for the outcomes I wanted. Due to the intensity of the battle, my praying finally collapsed and I admitted to myself that my incessant mutterings were useless. I was so weak from my own efforts and finally realized that I no longer needed to persistently pester God with my prayer repetitions. I finally succumbed to the fact that I was all prayed out and only had the strength to whisper one word in my helplessness, "Jesus" .

But, that one word was enough to declare:
"Jesus, I need you.
Jesus, You love me.
You are my Savior and I trust you."

The battle that my family faced is almost over now and we can see some blessings that came about as a result of it. The bond of love within my family is stronger than ever before, but best of all, members of my family who had doubted the very existence of God now attend church service on a regular basis and know Him personally.

I've been blessed to learn a very important lesson as well. When the next storm comes raging around me, I should not be afraid.

For, I can scream, "GOD, Please Help Me !" I can pray without ceasing. Or, I can simply whisper His name.

John 16:24 Until now you have asked for nothing in My name;
ask and you will receive,
so that your joy may be full.

Chapter 13

Designing The Project

Sometimes I card, spin and dye fiber, and let the yarn I produce inspire me. The colors, softness or other characters seem to speak to me and let me know if I should make a warm colorful hat or a delicate lacy scarf or shawl. Then, I search for a pattern or design one to bring out the yarn's best characteristics. More often, I plan a project completely before I begin processing any fiber.

I remember the year I fell in love with the hydrangea bush blooming in my mother's yard. Each massive blossom contained blue, pink, purple and white petals and the plant's leaves were a rich hunter green. With this in mind, I decided to knit what I call my hydrangea vest. I worked diligently at mixing the dyes to match the hues of the blossom's colors and used a photo from a gardening book as my reference guide. My dyeing method was also unique, because I wanted the colors to be sporadic rather than in large isolated pockets. The result was spectacular and I always think of my mother's garden whenever I wear it.

As I write this book, I am motivated to make something for myself to remind me about this writing project. I want the result to illustrate the Good Shepherd Farm as well as my love for Christ. With these themes in mind, I picture a unique cowl design that will include fair isle knitting of sheep, a heart and a cross. I've started looking on the internet for fair isle charts of these shapes and once I decide upon the size of the cowl, I will layout the charts on graph paper and create a pattern.

Since the cowl will be fair isle, which is a form of stranded knitting using multiple colors, I will line it, so the yarn floats on the reverse side of the knitting will be hidden. I've decided to knit the lining attached to the front and use a purl row to form a neatly folded edge.

One of the unique features of Sanquhar knitted gloves is that the recipients initials and the date they were knitted are embedded at the wrist of each glove. Sanquhar is a town in Scotland and is well known for it's unique and thriving knitting industry dating back to the 16th century. The gloves were knit with extremely fine wool yarn in stranded knitting, most often in black and white, and the knitting charts are still in use today. I find Sanquhar knitting patterns extremely appealing so I plan to incorporate the title of this book and the year written into my final design.

When my pattern notes are completed, I will be able to determine the yardage requirements for each of the colors I will need. The cowl will primarily be knit in wool, but I plan to add some angora fiber into the yarn to knit the sheep, which will give them a fluffy haze. In future planning of the project, I will consider if metallic fibers or beads will be used to add any additional appeal.

Yarn gauge is important and I will spin the yarn with a specific thickness in mind. The size of the knitting needles I select will ensure that I meet the desired stitches per inch.

As you can see there are a lot of steps in completing a unique knitting project. Fortunately, I knit for pleasure and am not under any time constraints of meeting a deadline. My enthusiasm for knitting this particular piece, which will tell my story, is driving me to proceed. It is my hope that it will spark interest and I will have an opportunity to share, not only my story of the Good Shepherd Farm, but my love of Christ as well.

Isaiah 64:8 But now, O LORD, Your are our Father,
We are the clay, and You our potter;
And all of us are the work of Your hand.

"Sanquhar Suzy"
Original Knitting Pattern by
Michelle Dumoulin

A Fair Isle hat inspired by the Sanquhar knitting designs of Scotland in a fingering weight yarn.

Yarn: Wool/angora blend hand spun yarn, burgundy (MC), white (CC) approximately 150 yards each color

Needles: 1 16" US 1.5 circular needle or dpns
            1 16" US 2.5 circular needle and set dpns
Notions: stitch markers, crochet hook or tapestry needle

ABBREVIATIONS:
st(s) - stitch(es)
k =   knit
p =   purl
m1=   make one stitch by picking up loop from the row below
k2tog= knit 2 stitches together
sl1,k1,psso = slip 1 as if to knit, k1, pass the slipped stitch
            over the knit stitch

DIRECTIONS:

Brim: On smaller needles, using MC cast on 132 sts.

- Prepare to join in the round, then cast on one extra stitch onto the right needle.
- Slip one stitch from the left needle (the beginning of the cast on) onto the right needle.
- Pass the extra cast on stitch over the slipped stitch, then slip that stitch back onto the left needle.
- Place marker to designate the beginning of the round.
- Break of MC, leaving a 2" tail for weaving in later.
- Using the CC, K2, P2, for 20 rows

Hat: Do not break off CC
        With MC, knit 2 rows around. (132 stitches)

Row 1: (k2, m1) around, using loop from the first stitch for your final m1. (198 stitches).

Row 2 - Row 44: Change to larger circular needle and knitting all stitches, work rows 2 through 22 of the chart, placing a marker after the last stitch of each pattern repeat. (9 pattern repeats)

Repeat chart, knitting rows 1 through 22 again.

Row 45: Knit row 45 of the chart, and make 2 stitches somewhere along the row, m1 near stitch 60 and then m1 near stitch 120. (200 stitches)
Remove the pattern repeat stitch markers, but not the marker designating the beginning of the round.

Crown Shaping:

Row 46 - Row 63: Follow chart for color changes, paying attention to the symbols designating K2tog or Sl1,K1,psso as indicated. (20 stitches) and changing to dpns as needed.

Row 64/65: K2tog around until 5 stitches remain, alternating yarn colors.

Break yarns, thread yarn tails through the remaining stitches. Pass the tail into the hole and pull tightly. Weave in all tails.Wet block and lay flat to dry.

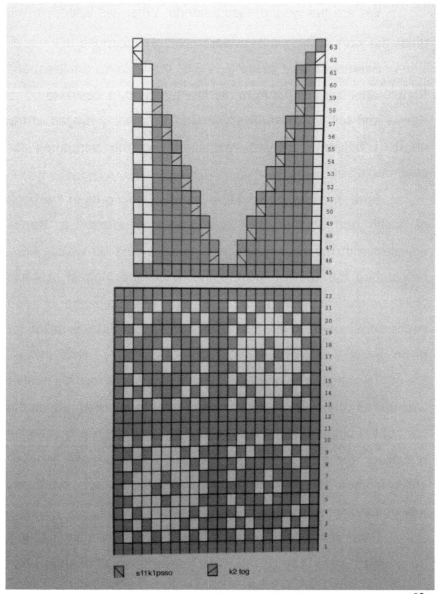

Chapter 14

God's Plan

We are the work of God's hands. When we listen, He will guide the work of our hands to accomplish His purpose.

Even as a very young girl I was drawn to be a missionary. Shortly after my divorce from my first husband, a desire to go to Kenya and tell the children about God wretchedly tugged at my heart. I diligently prayed and searched the scriptures for confirmation of His plan.

Sure enough, He spoke to me through words in the book of Isaiah and affirmed it. I contacted a missionary in Kenya affiliated with my church and was told I would be welcomed. I researched the cost of the trip, but knew the biggest obstacle would be convincing my family that I, now a single mother of three young sons, intended to travel across the globe and was called for this purpose. I was correct.

To my surprise, my Granny was supportive, but my mother was fearful of the whole idea and my aunt threatened to stand in front of the plane to stop me from leaving. Quickly, common sense prevailed, and I put to rest my vision of teaching those beautiful children about the love of God. But God's plan was eventually fulfilled by different means.

Five years later, early on a Sunday morning, I was overcome by the Holy Spirit to teach the message of what I had just read in my Bible to children that very day. When I got into my car, I was led to an African church that was attended by relatives of my former husband. I had never been there before and was unfamiliar with any of their church procedures.

Upon my arrival, I met a young boy and asked him to direct me to his Sunday School teacher. I was told the teacher's name and that he would be arriving shortly. I hovered around the classroom door and when the teacher arrived, quickly shared with him the events of that morning. I told him I was drawn to teach these children, so he left me, but returned a few minutes later to escort me into the classroom. He immediately called the children to order, said an opening prayer, and introduced me as their teacher for the day.

To say the Holy Spirit poured out of me is an understatement. As I paced in front of the room, I never knew what I was going to say next. The lesson was from the book of 1 John and repeated a message to "my little children" about loving one another and that Christ is our advocate for sin. There were approximately thirty children, ranging in age from elementary school to junior high, sitting cross-legged on the floor in absolute silence as I spoke. The Lord helped me to interpret the verses at a level they could understand.

As I stood there, and brought the lesson to an end, I envisioned my missionary desire and realized it was being fulfilled in that classroom that morning. Even today, I can remember the faces of those children staring at me with their utmost attention the entire time. A few times I've wondered if there was a specific purpose to that message for even one of those children, or where they are today.

Over the years, I doubted my understanding of the scripture verses from the Book of Isaiah and its guidance leading me to Kenya. But, more than twenty years after hearing that affirmation, I was shocked when a pastor introduced me to a missionary song quoting the same Bible verses. We sang that joyful song for our annual conference, welcoming missionaries from around the world.

I will always remember teaching those children and laughing with God as I was leaving the church, knowing that when He has a plan for my life, He will complete it!

Jeremiah 29:11 "For I know the plans that I have for you,"
declares the Lord,
"plans to prosper you and not to harm you,
plans to give you hope and a future."

Chapter 15

Dyeing Fiber

The number of ways fiber can be dyed are many, but not all fibers will accept color successfully. One of the main reasons that I love to use fibers from the farm is because they are natural fibers. Natural fibers such as wool, angora, alpaca, and cashmere can easily be dyed in a variety of methods, but I have never been able to dye synthetic fibers, such as acrylic.

A friend once gave me some material that was being discarded from a local manufacturing company, and while it was something I could spin, it never accepted any type of dye I applied and, therefore, it is still sitting in the attic unused. After trying unsuccessfully to identify the material content, I am uncomfortable using it for anything that would be worn as a garment because I'm afraid of its' toxicity! I prefer to only work with fibers that I am familiar and comfortable with.

I've had very little official training on dyeing fiber but there is a fiber festival soon where I hope to attend a training class. This type of class is always very popular with spinners because learning new methods of dyeing fiber is always fun and exciting. As I've mentioned earlier, the annual spin-in is a great resource to gather information. I spoke with other spinners and gleaned information from them, and purchased a book at one of the annual events. I've also learned by watching videos on the internet, of which they are almost endless. Most of all, I've learned to dye fiber through trial and error.

One of the most significant errors I made was when I initially started to dye fiber. Instead of natural dyes, I used dangerous and toxic artificial dyes and, because of my ignorance, I felt the effects in my nostrils and lungs. It's unfortunate that I did not grasp the dangers of using toxic dyes when I started out.

There are many methods of dyeing that are extremely safe and fun to do. Natural dyes, such as plants or vegetables produce a variety of beautiful colors. One of my favorite memories of using natural dyes is when I used tea. Although I had knit a shawl in pure white wool, I wanted to give it an antique look. Tea dyeing was just the trick to give it an aged appearance.

I'm more experienced at using synthetic or acid dyes now, but my first option is to determine if I can achieve the results using extremely safe methods, such as food coloring or Kool-Aid. These products are so safe to use that even children can lend a helping hand. I never use my chemical dyes when anyone else is present, and in fact, the pots and tools used for this method are designated for dyeing purposes only and removed from the kitchen immediately after completing the dyeing project.

All dyes need a mordant in order for color to be absorbed into the fiber and to avoid washing out or fading. I pre-soak either my fiber, yarn or knitted project in warm water with vinegar for about a half hour to open up the fibers. The vinegar acts as the mordant to ensure that my dye affixes permanently to the fiber. I also add vinegar again, directly into my dye bath, before adding the actual dyes to the pot.

68

Dyes can be applied to fiber or yarn in many ways. Yarn or fiber must be accessible to the dye in order to absorb it. Generally my fiber is placed into the dye bath loosely and my yarn is gathered into a very loose hank, rather than a tightly wound skein, whereby the dye would not penetrate to the center. If I want all the fiber to be one consistent color, then all the fiber is dropped into the dye bath at once.

When dyeing my hydrangea vest, I filled several water bottles with different dye colors I had diluted with water until I reached the tone of each of the colors I wanted. I poked a single hole in each of the bottle caps with a nail. Three skeins of yarn were laid out onto a table which was covered with saran wrap. Then I sprinkled the various dye colors all over the yarn where I specifically wanted the dye placement. Once the dye was applied, I wrapped each skein of yarn with more saran wrap and formed separate bundles. The bundles were steamed in a pot with a rack at the bottom to set the dyes.

I've also dyed fiber in mason jars in the microwave or in a crock pot. A variegated fiber or yarn is created when multiple dyes are added to the water bath. I've added yellow to one side of the pot and blue to the opposite. Although some of it will absorb those distinct colors, the fiber in the middle will be green as a result of the blended dyes. I've also used a syringe to inject different dye colors onto various locations of a batch of fiber or a skein of yarn. As you can see the possibilities are endless.

Rapid changes in temperature or agitation can cause the fibers to felt so handling of natural fibers is extremely important. When the water in my dye bath has simmered for approximately half an hour and the water is now clear of any dye color, I am assured the dye has been set. In order to avoid felting, I let the water cool down naturally. Once it has cooled to a warm temperature, I wash it gently in a sink of warm water with a touch of shampoo added. I rinse the item numerous times, and avoid excess handling.

To thoroughly remove the rinse water, I wrap the fiber in an old towel, drop it on the floor, and step all over it. My body weight pressure is greater than squeezing it with my hands! Then, I let it dry thoroughly before spinning or knitting.

My favorite time to dye fiber is in the middle of winter. Although the days may be gloomy, working with color makes me happy. One winter I dyed and spun about fifteen skeins of yarn in different colors. I loved each and every one of them but knew I didn't need fifteen different colored hats. Instead, I made my "sweater of many colors" in alternating rows of yellow, orange, purples and greens. As I knit the sweater, I was afraid I would look like a clown. Rather, when I walk into a room, people always compliment me and tell me it is beautiful and unique.

1 Peter 3:3-4 Your adornment must not be
merely external-braiding the hair,
and wearing gold jewelry, or putting on dresses;
but let it be the hidden person of the heart,
with the imperishable quality of a gentle and quiet spirit,
which is precious in the sight of God.

MY HYDRANGEA VEST

MY SWEATER OF MANY COLORS !

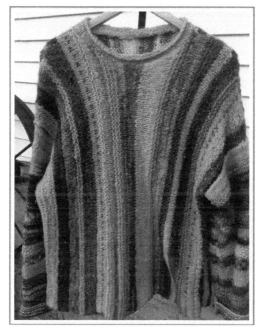

Chapter 16

The Angel

To say that my life as a single mom was extremely difficult is an understatement. My first husband was in and out of jail so many times due to his addiction to drugs and all the financial responsibilities were entirely mine to bear. For many years, I lived in fear, as a victim of his physical abuse.

One day, after that man was finally out of our lives for good, I was feeling unhappy and decided to replace the wallpaper in my son's bedroom to improve it for him. I had very little money, as always, but found some discount wallpaper at a bargain outlet for $1 per roll. It was white with a very small navy blue print and I knew it would brighten the room.

I purchased the number of rolls needed along with some wallpaper paste, but when I got to the last wall of the room, I ran out of paste. I stood there, leaning against that wall, and cried, because I only had $4 left to my name. Even so, I decided I was going to finish the project, and headed back to the store.

Tears were still falling down my face as I parked my car in the lot. As I walked into the store I was grateful it was raining and no-one would realize why my face was wet. After picking up one box of paste from the shelf, I went straight to the register to pay for it.

When I got to the cashier, there was a very old woman ahead of me in line. She was very tiny, no more than five feet tall, and wearing a long navy blue wool coat. The cashier scanned her items and told her the total amount due. Then, I overheard the woman respond that she didn't have enough money. She said she was short $1.50.

I looked at the counter and noticed she was buying very few items. In addition to a few cleaning supplies, she had three individual greeting cards. The cashier suggested she leave one of the cards behind, but the woman replied that she still wouldn't have enough.   So, the clerk suggested she eliminate a second one.

I realized she wasn't buying a box of miscellaneous cards. Rather, each of those cards was selected with a specific person in mind. I thought about the $4 I had in my pocket and knew that I only needed $1.50 of it. Quickly, I interrupted them, and said, "No, don't put those cards back, here is the money you need."

The cashier accepted my money and began putting the items in a bag.   The old woman then turned to me and asked, "May I have your address so I can mail the money to you?"

"No thank-you, that won't be necessary," I replied to her offer.

Then, she asked me, "What else can I do for you?"

I was still emotionally drained so I asked her, "Do you pray?"

She stood there smiling at me and her stare shook me to the core. I returned the stare and felt compelled to silently asked her, "Are you an angel?"

At that moment, while still holding her gaze on mine, she raised her hand and pointed to a tiny angel pin on the lapel of her coat. She nodded her head up and down a few times, as if answering me, "YES!" Then she turned around and picked up her bag and began walking very slowly towards the exit door.

It took me less than one minute to pay for my paste and I hurried to the door to catch up to her. When I exited the store, she was gone! She was nowhere in the parking lot getting into a vehicle and she also hadn't gotten into a car waiting at the entrance. There were no moving cars in sight.

As I slowly walked to my own car, I was certain she really was an angel and comforted to know she would talk to God and ask him to help me. I will never forget her, nodding her head, and pointing to the angel pin and consider our encounter a special blessing.

I wonder if there were other times an angel has been near me and I didn't recognize them.

Hebrews 13:2 Do not neglect to show hospitality to strangers,
for by this
some have entertained angels
without knowing it.

Chapter 17

Spinning

I love to spin fiber on my wheel. When done properly it's a peaceful rhythmic process and, while spinning, I think about how the yarn I am making will look when used in my knitting project.

My first decision is to choose the wheel I should use. As I've mentioned earlier, the Ashford spinning wheel is my favorite and has excellent tension control. If I am spinning a thin fingering weight yarn with extremely high quality fibers, then the Ashford is my obvious choice. On the other hand, if I am making a large quantity of a thicker yarn, then the Louet spinning wheel can be used. Either way, mastering the tension is the key to using each machine.

To start my project, I place an empty bobbin with a leader yarn onto the machine. The leader yarn is a piece of scrap yarn and should be at least a foot long. From the bobbin, the leader is drawn through yarn guides and out the orifice and I will start spinning my fiber onto it.

To summarize the process, my foot treadles the machine and spins the large drive wheel that spins the flyer. As the flyer spins, fiber is twisted and pulled onto the bobbin through the orifice, the hole in front of the machine. Both my spinning wheels are single treadle machines and therefore have only one foot pedal, but there are many types of double treadle spinning wheels whereby the spinner uses both feet.

Learning to spin requires doing three things at once and mastering each of them. Although there is a tension control knob, I control the machine by using both my hands and feet. My right foot treadles the machine at a comfortable and steady pace. The fingers of my left hand act as a stopper, releasing fibers into the orifice and limiting the twist. My right hand controls the amount of fiber that will be spun in a process called drafting. To me, the joy of spinning is achieved when these three steps are done in perfect harmony, working in a consistent rhythm to produce yarn that has uniformity of wraps per inch.

As I fill the bobbin, I am making a single strand of twisted fiber and always spin the drive wheel in a clockwise direction. Single ply yarn can be used for hats or scarfs but is not recommended for knitting items that will have wear and tear. I don't enjoy knitting with a single ply yarn because it produces a crooked stitch, which is called biased. I want my knitted items to be durable and always make my yarn with a minimum of two strands of spun fiber.

After filling two bobbins, I ply the strands together. When plying, the drive wheel is spun in a counter-clockwise direction to balance the twist of the yarn. The most important aspect of plying yarn is ensuring the twist in the counter-clockwise motion is equal to the twist of the original spun fiber.

I've learned different methods of plying yarn and do have a preference. One approach is to transfer the single strand off the bobbin into a ball, using a ball winder. I ply the strand from the

76

center of the ball with the strand on the outside. The benefit of plying these two ends together is that I will be able to ply all the fiber without any waste, plying until I reach the center.

I've also learned another plying method at one of the Annual Spin-Ins called navajo plying. Navajo plying produces a three ply yarn from a single strand and is best suited for making yarn that has striped color changes.

My preferred method is plying directly from bobbins held on a bobbin rack, called a lazy kate. In this method, I can easily control the tension. Bobbins spin freely and strands are drawn together as needed.

Sometimes, it takes hours, days or even weeks for me to spin all the yarn I need. Of course I could easily purchase yarn for knitting, but I love to spin my own yarn that is unique, unlike any other.

In the process of spinning my own fiber, I must face obstacles. Short second cuts, pieces of hay or even tangled locks must be handled quickly because the flyer is spinning at such a fast pace. As I spin, I hope for the best, but sometimes allow imperfectly spun yarn to pass through.

To me, spinning is a process of forgiveness as I accept my imperfections. I know that only Christ is perfect, but with the fruits of the Spirit, I press on to the goal.

Galatians 5:22-23 But the fruit of the Spirit is love, joy, peace, patience, kindness, goodness faithfulness, gentleness, self-control; against such things there is no law.

SPINNING YARN

Balanced Yarn on the Left
no twist in the skein

Unbalanced Yarn on the Right
twist in the skein

Chapter 18

The Fleece Story

It may appear that I was first introduced to fleece when my husband and I raised our own sheep on our Good Shepherd Farm, but, in fact, I want to tell you about a fleece story that happened before I moved to Maine.

Once I became a Christian, I decided I no longer wanted to follow my own heart's desires or lean on my own understanding. Rather, I wanted to seek direction from God and do His will, instead of my own. Although my intention was good, I made mistakes, but eventually I learned how to hear God's direction for my life clearly.

My initial strategy was to read my Bible with a particular concern in mind. As I read the scriptures, I searched for words or versus which I then interpreted as answers to my problem. Naively thinking I had received a divine revelation, I boldly set off on a new path, only to find when I got to the end of the road, failure. I experienced quite a bit of heartache those first few years. I'm a slow learner and tried this method a few times before realizing I needed a new approach.

The next method was similar, but I added prayers for understanding, before I read the Word. Confident the Holy Spirit was guiding me, I made decisions, but continued to find I was wrong again. Looking back on those years, it was foolish of me to manipulate the Word of God for my own personal goals. I realize I had not fully surrendered my personal desires and within a year of my marriage to Gary I faced a huge decision.

We lived in a four bedroom home in a really nice area of the city and our families lived nearby. Drastically, a few events occurred that caused us to consider moving, not next door, but out of the State.

First, as I learned more about my new husband, I realized he was not happy. He had grown up on a farm in a rural area. Our home was in a city, and the traffic congestion was just one issue he hated. Secondly, there was an increasing problem of drug use in the area. I worried that my sons would get influenced down that horrid path. Lastly, the event of September 11th happened in New York. As the crow flies, living near Cape Cod is a short distance from Boston, and I was afraid my family would be hurt if such an event happened there.

We had spent our honeymoon in a cottage my sister owned in Maine and loved the area. During that first year of marriage, we also travelled to Arizona to visit his father. As we casually talked about moving, we considered both of these locations. As much as we loved the northern Arizona terrain, I was adamant that it was too far from my family, and therefore, out of the question. On the other hand, Maine was within our reach. Both of these areas only became options after researching farmland near our current home, but land prices were astronomical and out of range of what we could afford.

As we spent time haphazardly looking at property in Maine on the internet, we learned that land prices were extremely

80

reasonable. Eventually, we visited our current home with a realtor and decided it would be a great location to start a small farm. Unfortunately, my children did not want to move. So the final decision was for me to make and it was a big one.

I felt extremely heavy burdened. Although I had made decisions that turned out best for my family, I had also made mistakes. I realized I deceived myself in my previous attempts to get clear direction from God. Too often, my interpretation of His Word was influenced by my desires. Satan as well, who is the Master of Deception, had led me astray from the Truth.

This time, more than ever, I wanted to be absolutely certain of God's will and searched my Bible for direction. I found my answer in the sixth chapter of the Book of Judges, versus 36 to 40:

Sign of the Fleece.

36 Then Gideon said to God, "If You will deliver Israel through me, as You have spoken, 37 behold, I will put a fleece of wool on the threshing floor. If there is dew on the fleece only, and it is dry on all the ground, then I will know that You will deliver Israel through me, as You have spoken." 38 And it was so. When he arose early the next morning and squeezed the fleece, he drained the dew from the fleece, a bowl full of water. 39 Then Gideon said to God, "Do not let Your anger burn against me that I may speak once more; please let me make a test once more with the fleece, let it now be dry only on

the fleece, and let there be dew on all the ground."
40 God did so that night; for it was dry only on the
fleece, and dew was on all the ground.

It was very clear to me that Gideon was not testing God's abilities in any way. He heard God speak to him but wanted to know with certainty God's plan. God heard his request and in the morning the ground was dry and the fleece was wet. Gideon second guessed himself and still doubted his own abilities to be sure. He begged God to communicate with him once again. Sure enough, the next morning, the fleece was dry and the ground was wet.

That's where I was, just like Gideon, wanting to know clear direction from God if we should move to Maine. I didn't have a fleece and using one never actually occurred to me. Instead, I asked God to show me clear direction another way.

I met with a realtor, settled on the selling price and signed the contract. But as I closed the door behind her, I immediately asked the Lord for guidance, and put the final decision in His hands. As the words flowed from my mouth, I placed my two fleece on the threshing floor at the same time.

> *"Lord, if You sell my house,*
> *within one week,*
> *for the amount I am asking,*
> *I will know we should move."*

As expected, my children were anxious, and kept asking me for my decision. I told them I was praying about it and waiting for an answer. During that week, I was the only one at peace in our home because I had released it into His hands.

Our church was holding their Annual Christian Camp and every day I went to the campground early each morning to join others in morning prayer. I didn't dwell on the sale of my house in those morning prayers. In fact, I hardly thought about it. Then, the unthinkable happened. Within the week there was a buyer willing to pay the full price.

I remember going to camp the morning I heard the news and cried my eyes out. It was not the answer I wanted to hear. I cried my heart out to my pastor too, but I knew I had made an agreement with God and the decision was not debatable. I had asked Him what to do and had no choice but to obey. For the first time, I had completely surrendered to God's will.

Then, within a month of moving to Maine my world spun out of control rapidly as my two oldest sons decided to move back to live with family. There was nothing I could do as these young adults who had been the focus of my life as a single mother moved away from me. I missed them terribly every day and for the past fifteen years I've prayed to sell this property so I can be closer to them again.

They are grown men now with families of their own and God has still not answered this prayer request with the result I want to hear. As I walk with God, I continue to trust Him, regardless of the outcome, but continue to seek understanding of His plan.

Every so often I reflect on this transition and try to understand His purpose.

Perhaps He moved us to save my youngest child from a disaster.

Perhaps He put someone in my path who needed to be led to Him through me.

Perhaps He wanted me to grow closer to Him through adversities I've experienced here.

Perhaps He wanted me on the Good Shepherd Farm so I would write this book.

Perhaps, He moved me here for you in some way?

I don't know the reason, but I reply.
"OK Lord."

Isaiah 55: "For my thoughts are not your thoughts,
Nor are your ways My ways," declares the Lord.
"For as the heavens are higher than the earth,
So are My ways higher than your ways
And My thoughts than your thoughts."

Chapter 19

Final Processing

The most exciting moment of making my own yarn is close at hand and soon I will be able to see the characteristics of the final product. The moment of truth will arrive when I look at my yarn in the form of a hank.

In order to do that, I continue to ply the yarn strands together onto a new bobbin. When a bobbin is full, I manually wrap the yarn onto a tool called a niddy noddy. Then, it is in the form of a hank.

While most spinners use the standard shaped tool, I have a personalized niddy noddy which my husband invented and made just for me. Gary designed it so that one complete revolution around the path of my niddy noddy measures two yards. So, while I am winding the yarn onto the noddy noddy, I'm able to calculate my total yardage by counting the number of revolutions, then doubling the result.

My husband's gift to me was extremely thoughtful and kind. It works fantastic, is extremely portable, and stores well in my tool basket. One year, he made extras and sold them at our annual spin-in, but mine will always be unique and special. In the final process of varnishing the wood, he embedded photos of some of my sheep on the center panel.

I always laugh when I see the photo of Corrie. She is chewing hay, her mouth is distorted and she reminds me of the talking horse Mr. Ed!

After I've finished winding the yarn into a hank, I secure it in a few places with a few small pieces of scrap yarn so it doesn't get tangled. The moment of truth arrives when I remove the hank from the niddy noddy and let it hang freely from my hand. I will immediately know if the yarn twist is balanced by how it hangs. An unbalanced hank of yarn twists back onto itself like a coil or spring. An unbalanced twist can sometimes be corrected by hanging weights on it during the drying process but I love it when the hank drops loosely from my hand!

The next process is to soak the yarn in warm soapy water with a little shampoo to set the twist permanently. I am extremely careful with the water temperature and handling of the yarn to avoid felting. Using an old towel, I squeeze out any excess water and hang the hank of yarn to dry on a wooden quilt rack.

When it has completely dried, it needs to be transferred a final time into balls for knitting. There are two more tools needed for this final procedure; a yarn swift and a ball winder. My yarn swift is a tool that simply expands like an umbrella and holds the hank of yarn in place. The umbrella rotates freely around a central rod while I manually operate the crank handle of my ball winder. The yarn is wrapped onto the winder around a central core. Once the yarn is wrapped, I remove it carefully.

At last, I have the final product I have been working towards and it can be stored away until I am ready to start my knitting project. It has been a long journey to reach this point and, when I look back on the process, I have wonderful memories.

I rarely think about the work involved from raising the sheep to spinning the fiber. Rather, I remember the hour upon hour in which I abided in the presence of the Holy Spirit, dwelt upon His Word or prayed.

John 15: 4 Abide in Me, and I in you.
As the branch cannot bear fruit of itself unless it abides in the vine,
so neither can you unless you abide in Me.

Tools

From Left, clockwise:

- A ball of yarn, after it has been removed from the ball winder.

- Lazy Kate, the bottom bobbin has a leader yarn

- Yarn swift

- Ball winder

- My Niddy Noddy!

Chapter 20

Financial Miracle #1

I confess that I did not always tithe ten percent of my income to the church, but when I did, it was done for the purpose of being obedient to God's Word and not with an ulterior motive of personal blessings. Without fail, God has always been true to His Word and supplied all of my needs.

On at least three specific occasions, God supplied more than the everyday needs of my children and me. Through some of the darkest hours of my life, when I was totally helpless, He performed financial miracles. In each case, the results were improbable and only achieved because of His divine intervention. These were not minor financial burdens. In fact, the first miracle happened when I was about to lose our home for nonpayment of the mortgage.

Not surprisingly, my first husband left with every bill in the house overdue. I was totally overwhelmed when the mortgage company sent me a letter stating they needed $1200 within a month to avoid foreclosure. Working as an accountant, I kept to a strict budget in order to keep the lights turned on and put whatever food I could manage on the table. I knew it would be impossible to come up with that much money and I feared losing the roof over our heads.

When the day of my meeting at the finance office arrived I had only scraped together $1,000, money which was desperately needed to pay other bills. As I walked up the granite stairs of the building, with my shoulders slumped, I had very little strength to plead for mercy. I had never been to this building before nor spoken with anyone in this office. In fact, it was all strange to me when I was asked to be seated at the desk of the woman who handled my mortgage account.

Within the first minute of our meeting I told her I was sorry but could only pay $1,000 of the overdue amount. I also explained that I intended to sell the house and pay off the entire mortgage balance at that time.

In response, she said that she knew I was a very nice person and would be willing to wait for the delinquent payments until the house was sold. Our entire meeting lasted five minutes and I never pulled the envelope of money entirely out of my purse!

I will always remember descending those granite steps, returning home with the money that was not enough to stop the foreclosure and laughing with joy at the wonder and amazement of God's favor.

Genesis 18: 14 Is anything too difficult for the Lord?

"FAITH"
Original Knitting Pattern by
Michelle Dumoulin

This shawl was designed to show the beauty of the colors of my hand-spun yarn project. It is an asymmetrical triangular shape and can easily be adapted for size alterations.

The shawl is composed of three stitch patterns; the andalusian stitch, the granite relief stitch and the garter stitch. The number of row repeats of each stitch pattern were varied to enhance its' beauty.

The options of yarn choice, color and stitch pattern repeats are endless, allowing you to create your own unique design. So step out in faith and you will not be disappointed.

"Now faith is the assurance of things hoped for, the conviction of things not seen." Hebrews 1:11

Yarn:
- Approximately 350 yards of fingering weight wool hand-spun yarn as follows:

    - 100 yards dark variegated color (Color A)
    - 100 yards solid light color (Color B)
    - 150 yards light variegated color (Color C)

    Or any fingering to sport weight yarn in any color(s) of your choice.

- Hand Made Goodshepfarm Knitting Needles Size 8

- Gauge: 14 stitches per 4 inches;
    3.5 stitches per inch when wet blocked vigorously

- Completed Dimensions: 87" by 18"

Abbreviations:

st =	stitches
K =	knit
P =	purl
YO =	Yarn over
K1 =	knit 1 stitch
K2 =	knit 2 stitches
K3 =	knit 3 stitches
K to 1st =	knit until 1 stitch remains
K to last3 =	knit until 3 stitches remain
K all =	knit all remaining stitches
P to 1st=	purl until 1 stitch remains
K1,P1 =	knit 1 stitch, then purl 1 stitch
K2tog =	Knit 2 stitches together
KFB =	Knit into the front of the stitch as usual, then also knit into the back loop of the same stitch
RS =	Right side
WS =	Wrong side

Cast on 3 st with Color A.

RS	Row 1:	K1, YO, K2
WS	Row 2:	K all (4 st)
RS	Row 3:	K1, YO, K3
WS	Row 4:	K all (5 st)
RS	Row 5:	K1, YO, K1, K2tog, K1
WS	Row 6:	K to 1st, YO, K1
RS	Row 7:	K1, YO, K2, K2tog, K1
WS	Row 8:	K to 1st, YO, K1
RS	Row 9:	K1, YO, K to last3, K2tog, K1
WS	Row 10:	K2tog until 1 stitch remains, YO, K1
RS	Row 11:	K1, YO, KFB until 2 stitches remain, K2
WS	Row 12:	P to 1st, YO, K1
RS	Row 13:	K1, YO, K to last3, K2tog, K1
WS	Row 14:	P to 1st, YO, K1
RS	Row 15:	K1, YO, *K1, P1* until 3 st remain, K2tog, K1
WS	Row 16:	P to 1st, YO, K1

Repeat rows 9 to 16 - 7 more times
Then repeat row 9 and row 12 once (Row 74, 40 stitches)

Change to Color B:

RS	Row 75:	K1, YO, K to last3, K2tog, K1
WS	Row 76:	K to 1st, YO, K1
RS	Row 77:	K1, YO, K to last3, K2tog, K1
WS	Row 78:	P to 1st, YO, K1

RS	Row 79:	K1, YO, K all
WS	Row 80:	K2tog until 1 stitch remains, YO, K1
RS	Row 81:	K1, YO, KFB until 2 stitches remain, K2
WS	Row 82:	P to 1st, YO, K1
RS	Row 83:	K1, YO, K to last3, K2tog, K1
WS	Row 84:	P to 1st, YO, K1
RS	Row 85:	K1, YO, *K1, P1* until 3 st remain, K2tog, K1
WS	Row 86:	P to 1st, YO, K1

RS	Row 87:	K1, YO, K all
WS	Row 88:	K to 1st, YO, K1
RS	Row 89:	K1, YO, K to last3, K2tog, K1
WS	Row 90:	P to 1st, YO, K1

Change to Color C:

Rows 91 to 98:	Repeat rows 79 to 86
Rows 99 to 102:	Repeat rows 87 to 90
Rows 103 to 106:	Repeat rows 79 to 82 (Row 106, 61 st)

Change to Color A:

RS	Row 107:	K1, YO, K to last3, K2tog, K1
WS	Row 108:	K2tog until 1 stitch remains, YO, K1
RS	Row 109:	K1, YO, KFB until 2 stitches remain, K2
WS	Row 110:	P to 1st, YO, K1

Repeat rows 107 to 110 - 3 more times (Row 122, 69 stitches)

94

Change to Color C:
RS   Row 123:   K1, YO, K to last3, K2tog, K1
WS   Row 124:   P to 1st, YO, K1
RS   Row 125:   K1, YO, *K1, P1* until 3 st remain, K2tog, K1
WS   Row 126:   P to 1st, YO, K1
Repeat rows 123 to 126 - 3 <u>more</u> times (Row 138, 77 stitches)

Change to Color B:
RS   Row 139:   K1, YO, K to last3, K2tog, K1
WS   Row 140:   P to 1st, YO, K1

RS   Row 141:   K1, YO, K all
WS   Row 142:   P to 1st, YO, K1

Rows 143 to 146:   Repeat rows 139 and 140 <u>twice</u>

RS   Row 147:   K1, YO, K to last3, K2tog, K1
WS   Row 148:   K to 1st, YO, K1
RS   Row 149:   K1, YO, K all
WS   Row 150:   K to 1st, YO, K1

Row 151 to 154:   Repeat rows 147 to 150
Rows 155 to 158:   Repeat rows 139 and 140 <u>twice</u>
Rows 159 to 166:   Repeat rows 147 to 150 <u>twice</u>
Rows 167 to 168:   Repeat rows 139 and 140 (ending with 97
          stitches)

Change to Color A:
Rows 169 to 176:   Repeat rows 9 to 16

Change to Color C:
Rows 177 to 184:   Repeat rows 9 to 16
Rows 185 to 200:   Repeat rows 9 to 12 <u>four times</u>
Rows 201 to 204:   Repeat rows 13 to 16
Row 205:   Repeat row 9
Row 206:   Repeat row 6 (ending with 116 stitches)

Bind-off using the following method to ensure the cast-off edge is not puckered.

- Insert needle in front to pick up 2 stitches
- Wrap the yarn around the needle clockwise and knit the two together loosely
- Return that stitch to the left needle and repeat until only one stitch remains.
- Slip the tail through the final stitch and tighten the loop.

Housekeeping:

Weave in the tails, hand wash the garment then block vigorously with pins to stretch to its' length capacity. Allow to dry completely.

Chapter 21

Fair Isle Knitting

One of my favorite knitting styles is Fair Isle knitting. When done properly, I always feel a sense of accomplishment when my knitting project is completed. Although true Fair Isle knitting refers to color work patterns which are specific to the Shetland Islands, many knitters like myself use this term to refer to any "stranded color work" that creates patterns using two strands of yarn of different colors in a single row of knitting.

Although I do a lot of knitting, I find I most often get compliments on items I knit in my Fair Isle technique. A few years ago, I posted a photograph of a pair of socks on an international knitting forum of which I am a member. I was surprised when other knitters from around the world said the floats of my fair isle knitting were impeccable! My Fair Isle knitting certainly didn't start out successfully. In fact, the first hat I knit in this method wouldn't even stretch over my head!

I never attended a formal knitting class so I developed my own procedures and consider them all equally important. To summarize my Fair Isle knitting method, I designate each yarn as the main or contrasting color and maintain the yarn's knitting position in relationship to the needle, especially after anchoring the floats. By using an anchoring pattern and a consistent direction, I am able to maintain an even tension.

As I alternate knitting with each of the two strands of yarn, I always consider one of the strands the MC (Main Color) and the other strand as the CC (Contrasting Color). In my method, each of these colors maintains their position in relationship to the working knitting needle. The Main Color is always knit closest to the needle using my pointer finger, and the Contrasting Color yarn is always worked from behind the Main Color, knit using my middle finger.

I usually follow a chart that shows the color requirement of each stitch. In order to keep track, I use post-it-note stickers and align them under the row I am currently knitting, moving the sticky note paper up the chart as each row is completed.

Since each stitch is knit using only one of the two strands, the yarn not in use is dropped and carried along the back of the knitting until needed again. The distance between stitches that the yarn is dropped is called the float. Based on the pattern, a strand of yarn may need to float quite a long distance and I find that is undesirable for many reasons. Long unknit yarns hanging across the back of my knitting could be snagged and also looks very untidy. If I have long floats, I find it difficult to maintain a consistent knitting tension and tend to pull the yarn too tightly when bringing it back into play as my working yarn.

As a solution, I developed a systematic procedure to anchor my stitches with the working yarn and eliminate long floats. To avoid them, I never carry a float behind my knitting further than three stitches without anchoring it by the yarn in use. When anchoring the main color, I always wrap the yarn around the contrasting color in a clockwise direction. To anchor the contrasting color, it is wrapped around the main color counter-clockwise.

I also developed the following chart to anchor my floats in a consistent manner.

<u>Anchoring Chart</u>:
4 Stitch Float: knit 2, anchor, knit 2
5 Stitch Float: knit 2, anchor, knit 3
6 Stitch Float: knit 3, anchor, knit 3
7 Stitch Float: knit 2, anchor, knit 2, anchor, knit 3
8 Stitch Float: knit 2, anchor, knit 3, anchor, knit 3
and so on....

The training my Granny gave me as a child is engrained in me. I remember that she loved the Apostle Peter and used a Bible verse from the Book of 1 Peter in my training. She talked to me about this reading from chapter 3;

"Your adornment must not be merely external-braiding the hair,
and wearing gold jewelry, or putting on dresses;
but let it be the hidden person of the heart,
with the imperishable quality of a gentle and quiet spirit,
which is precious in the sight of God."

Granny taught me not to look at outward appearances and character is revealed through words and behavior. She also taught me that the hidden side of any garment must always be ready for inspection as well! Therefore, I developed these knitting procedures so the inside of my knitting will always be tidy.

Proverbs 31: 30 Charm is deceitful and beauty is vain,
But a woman who fears the Lord, she shall be praised.

Fair-Isle Knitted Items

Chapter 22

Financial Miracle #2

When I returned from the mailbox and passed through the kitchen, I threw the entire stack of bills into my Bible lying on the kitchen table. I abandoned them and immediately walked away, acknowledging it would be totally impossible to pay them now. Never imagining the situation would change in just a few minutes, I proceeded down the stairs to fold some laundry.

Standing at my folding table, I wasn't thinking about those bills or anything else for that matter. The doctor I had been seeing for a few months couldn't even understand how I was coping with the stress of a violent ex-husband. She expressed concern that I would soon have a physical or emotional breakdown. To avoid that, I quit my job, without a plan for my financial responsibilities.

It was quite peaceful and quiet as I folded the laundry in the basement. The children were at school and I was alone in the house. The only sound I could hear was the dryer tossing around more clothes. Then, for the second time in my life, I heard God speak to me.

I recognized His voice immediately and wasn't frightened or surprised. I was walking with the Lord, praying to Him constantly and reading His Word. His voice sounded like it was coming from the ceiling and I didn't clearly understand. So, I looked up, and casually asked, "What did You say?"

He spoke again. This time I heard Him say, "Disability Insurance." That possibility had never crossed my mind and I immediately wondered if I had medical insurance coverage to financially assist me through this difficult time.

I ran up the stairs, sat on the edge of my bed and telephoned my health insurance provider. After a brief explanation, the representative actually thanked me for calling him. He said that I did have insurance which would cover me retroactively to my last date of employment. I was also told I would receive a check in the mail in just a few days.

As soon as I ended the call, I went to the kitchen and looked through the bills I had placed in my Bible. Not only were they smaller amounts than I had expected, God had immediately made a way for them to be paid.

Deuteronomy 8:16 He humbled you and let you be hungry,
and fed you with manna which you did not know,
nor did your fathers know,
that He might make you understand
that man does not live by bread alone,
but man lives by everything that proceeds
out of the mouth of the LORD.

Chapter 23

Blocking

When Granny taught me sewing, every step in the process involved ironing. Seams were ironed open before attaching another layer, darts were pressed to the side where they would lay permanently, and the garment was pressed, over and over again. I was recently surprised to learn that a coworker did not even own an iron. Instead, she uses the wrinkle release cycle of her clothes dryer for this purpose.

Granny also told me to wash every knit or crochet item I made, especially if it was going to be given as a gift. Caring for acrylic yarn was easy since most items could be washed in the machine, thrown in the dryer, or laid flat to dry.

When I began knitting with wool and natural fibers, I needed to learn how to obtain results similar to my previous washing and ironing methods. Blocking is the technique I use on natural fibers to stretch and evenly redistribute the final knitting stitches. It gives me professional results.

In earlier chapters I discussed how the fiber was washed numerous times; as a fleece directly off the sheep, during the dyeing process, and again after spun into yarn. Once again, after the item has been knitted, I wash it again, keeping a consistent water temperature. The water should be warm, not hot nor cold, for both washing and rinsing. I don't want the item to felt so avoid excessive handling. To avoid stretching, I never let the item hang wet from my hands, but support it by cupping it from underneath at all times.

As I fill the sink with the warm water, I squirt a small amount of shampoo into the water and swish it around gently to make bubbles. I prefer to use inexpensive shampoo that smells really nice, because I like the scent that lingers in my finished product. When the water level is sufficient, I press the garment down into the water and let it soak for at least 15 minutes. After soaking in this wash cycle, I remove the item from the water by lifting it out of the water, cupping it from below. While running the faucet with warm water, I quickly rinse the item of surface suds while squeezing gently. Then I drain and rinse the sink.

Once again, I fill the sink with water of the same temperature and allow the item to soak in the rinse cycle. After another brief period of time, I lift the item from the water carefully, and rinse and squeeze it thoroughly but gently under warm running water, until all the suds are removed.

To start the drying process, I lay the garment flat, without stretching, onto an old bath towel I save for this purpose. Starting on one end, I roll the towel up into a tube shape, with the knitted item in it. After laying the tube gently on the floor, I step all over it, removing all the excess water from my knitted piece. When I unroll the towel, I am often surprised to find that my item feels almost completely dry.

For small items, I then lay it onto my ironing board which has been covered by a folded sheet. For larger items I use the spare bed for blocking. Using my hands, I press it out, gently forming it into my desired shape. Sometimes, I stretch and pull the stitches into the final shape I want and pin it into place. Items knit in a lace patterns look fantastic when pinned and stretched to display the lace design stitches.

I let it dry for at least 24 hours. Of course, during that time, I look at it often, and enjoy how the stitches have settled neatly in the process. When one side is dry, I turn it over, to finish drying thoroughly.

I know I've confessed to being a yarn snob, and will now confess that I'm a blocking snob as well. I block everything I knit. It saddens me to see beautiful items knit by others that are not blocked. Edges that roll up, rather than laying flat and neat, and a finished product that looks wrinkled could easily be avoided by this simple process.

Only when asked for my advice or opinion will I suggest blocking. I don't want to cast judgement on other knitters but instead prefer to offer them praise for their accomplishments.
How can I be critical of others? There are so many knitters with more expertise and I still have techniques to learn.

1 Corinthians 13:4 Love is patient,
love is kind and is not jealous;
love does not brag
and is not arrogant

Blocking a shawl on a spare bed

The shawl is stretched and pinned

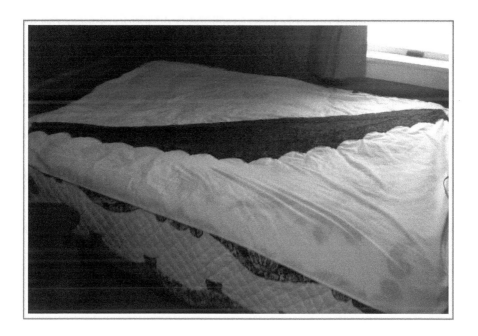

Chapter 24

Financial Miracle #3

That devil not only tried to kill me but tried to destroy me to the very end. The day before my scheduled meeting at the bank, to sign documents selling my first home, I received astonishing information from my attorney. The final title search revealed a surprising mortgage debt on my property. My ex-husband had borrowed $6,000 from his girlfriend and used the house as collateral for that loan. In order to proceed with the sale, I needed her to release me of that financial obligation.

The girlfriend was a complete stranger, in fact, I didn't know her name or address. Through research, the lawyer provided me with that information and told me that I needed her to sign a "release of lien" document in the presence of a notary public.

By the time I left work, daylight had already passed. First, I went home to tend to the children, then drove to the address I was given. I sat outside her house in my car, getting the courage to approach the door of this stranger. It was cold, and it was dark, and I prayed.

When I knocked on the door, a woman answered who confirmed she was the person I was seeking. As I stood on the doorstep, I introduced myself, told her what I had learned, and asked her to release me of his debt. I explained that I needed the money as a down payment to purchase another home for my children and myself.

She hesitated at my request and I could see she was frustrated and wanted to close the door in my face. But, just before she walked away, she asked me a question, "Why should I do this for you?"

To this day, I remember my response. I told her, if she did me this favor, I was certain God would bless her.

She immediately agreed to help and told me to meet her at a nearby notary office. At this time of night, with only minutes to spare, the office was still open and had the form she needed to sign. As we stood at the counter, both the notary and I were amazed as we witnessed this stranger sign a document releasing me of this debt.

The next day, I arrived at the bank, and learned the signed document in my hand was sufficient to proceed as planned. I submitted the form and thought about the stranger, confident she would be blessed.

Genesis 12:3 And I will bless those who bless you,
And the one who curses you I will curse.

Chapter 25

The Choice

My twin grandsons were less than a year old when my son called me in a panic. "Mom, Marcus is burning up!"

Ready to rush to the rescue, I ran outside and stood by my car. Pressing the phone tighter to my ear, I listened to him shouting to me about the condition of my grandchild. "I'm rushing him to the hospital now, but Mom, I'm scared. His temperature is 104 and his body feels so hot!"

"What hospital are you going to?", I managed to ask him. But, I didn't get a response. Instead, I heard, "I'll call you," before he abruptly hung up and his voice was gone.

For a brief moment, I contemplated barreling down the highway, but knew enough not to react to those instincts. It would be wiser for me to wait for him to call me with an update. If Marcus' condition did not improve or worsened, I would immediately begin the 4 1/2 hour trip.

I looked at the barn, and sighed, thinking of the possibility I may need to leave the animals once again. I imagined the disappointment my husband would feel if I left in haste and dropped the responsibilities of the farm on him once more. My shoulders slumped with the weight of heaviness as I acknowledged how often I had recently done just that.

I remembered when I had driven down to Massachusetts as soon as I received the news my daughter in law was in labor, and the twins were about to be born. Shortly after I left home, Gary called to tell me that Jeannette had lambed. I was sad because I had missed sharing that experience with my husband.

Not only did I miss the animals, but every time I left the farm I was concerned about their safety as well. Gary's job required that he travel all over the state, but I was never further than a few miles from home. If an emergency happened, everyone in town knew how to reach me.

As I stood in the driveway, I realized I had reached a critical moment. As much as the idea saddened me, I could no longer handle being torn by the choice of seeing my grandchildren or taking care of the farm. I went inside the house and told my husband of my decision to sell the sheep.

Jeannette, Corrie and Greedy were the last to go. Mistakingly I thought we could just downsize, so the rest of the flock was sold first. Unfortunately, in reality, reducing the size of the flock did not eliminate the responsibility on the farm. My favorite sheep still needed food and water on a daily basis, but letting them go was awful.

I remember loading them into the truck. They went willingly because they trusted me and followed the handful of grain I offered. But, after they left, throughout the evening, I visited the barn numerous times and cried until I was spent.

The sadness is only a memory now, because I consider myself abundantly blessed.

God not only blessed me with children and grandchildren, but with the love of my husband, I experienced the life and love we shared on the Good Shepherd Farm.

Psalm 23:1-3

The Lord is my shepherd,

I shall not want.

He makes me lie down in green pastures;

He leads me beside quiet water.

He restores my soul.

My Heart Still Lies
in the Shadow of
The Good Shepherd Farm

Epilogue

Yearning for the Sheep

Without the responsibility of the farm, Gary and I have been able to travel a few times together. In fact, since my job ended earlier this year, my loving husband encourages me to frequently visit my family. He recognizes that time with my mom, children and family is precious.

Of course I still miss the sheep. Every so often, I have a strong desire to restore the farm to what it once was, but I know in reality we won't do it, and we shouldn't. Instead, I wrote what I could remember about it in this book. I wanted to share my wonderful memories of it with you.

I must tell you that writing some of these chapters was agonizing. As expected, it was painful for me to remember some of the suffering I went through. I persevered though, because I wanted to desperately tell you about the greatness of our God.

It saddens me greatly to know there are people who deny Him, because I know their fate. But, God proved Himself to me and I wanted to share that proof with you.

Some people don't understand me and say I'm "over the top" or "deeply religious," but I don't mind. Wouldn't you be different if you Heard the Sound of Heaven, the Voice of God, or whisper His name every day?

My husband, Gary, loves Jesus too. Together, we named it "The Good Shepherd Farm" because of our love for Our Savior. The Bible tells us that Jesus Christ is the Good Shepherd who laid down His life for us, His sheep.

Sadly though, He also said the following in John 10:16:

"I have other sheep,
which are not of this fold;
I must bring them also,
and they will hear My voice;
and they will become one flock
with one shepherd.

I pray that if you are one of the other sheep, you respond to His voice.

He is yearning for YOU to join the flock.

I would appreciate your comments and would

love to hear from you..........

Contact me by email at:
goodshepfarm@mainestream.us

Facebook or Instagram at:
Goodshepfarm

Visit me at my
Goodshepfarm Shop on Etsy
to purchase additional copies
or other knitting or spinning products

Thank you

Yarns from
My Shepherd
MICHELLE DUMOULIN

The Lord is my Shepherd

He restores my soul

Index to Knitting Patterns

118